5-Star Review by Readers' Favorite

Human Resource Management Essentials You Always Wanted To Know by Jaquina Gilbert is a handy manual that gives basic information about Human Resource Management as both a management function and an operating department within an organization. The purpose of the book is to help readers understand the definition, the evolutionary progress, basic functions, opposing viewpoints, and challenges of Human Resource Management. HRM is a simple scheme that employs policies, practices, and systems to close the gaps between the company, management, and staff. This book gives a good description of all aspects, concepts, and application of the topic, helping readers to learn more about HRM.

People form the core of any company and the book features several approaches to HRM with its unique viewpoints. The approach to the topic is simple and structured, making it easy for readers to comprehend, and the author's experience and examples make it an engaging read. The book works as a good manual for readers who want to pursue a career in Human Resource Management and also for current HR professionals. Employer-Employee relationships can be complicated and the book gives techniques and tools to protect the relationship which plays a key role in the success of any organization. Jaquina Gilbert looks at the Pre-Industrial Revolution, the Industrial Revolution (1750-1850), and the Post-Industrial Revolution (1850), and the various theories of Human Resource Management, thereby giving readers useful information. It is a must-read and must-have for all those readers who have a Human Resource Management background and to those who are interested in the topic and want to have a career in it.

This review is for an earlier edition.

SELF-LEARNING MANAGEMENT SERIES

HUMAN RESOURCE MANAGEMENT ESSENTIALS

YOU ALWAYS WANTED TO KNOW

JAQUINA GILBERT

VIBRANT
PUBLISHERS

Human Resource Management Essentials

You Always Wanted To Know

Paperback ISBN 10: 1-949395-83-9
Paperback ISBN 13: 978-1-949395-83-9

Ebook ISBN 10: 1-949395-84-7
Ebook ISBN ISBN 13: 978-1-949395-84-6

Hardback ISBN 10: 1-949395-85-5
Hardback ISBN 13: 978-1-949395-85-3

Library of Congress Control Number: 2020933928

This publication is designed to provide accurate and authoritative information in regard to the subject matter covered. The Author has made every effort in the preparation of this book to ensure the accuracy of the information. However, information in this book is sold without warranty either expressed or implied. The Author or the Publisher will not be liable for any damages caused or alleged to be caused either directly or indirectly by this book.

Vibrant Publishers books are available at special quantity discount for sales promotions, or for use in corporate training programs. For more information please write to bulkorders@vibrantpublishers.com

Please email feedback / corrections (technical, grammatical or spelling) to spellerrors@vibrantpublishers.com

To access the complete catalogue of Vibrant Publishers, visit www.vibrantpublishers.com

What experts say about this book!

"Human Resource Management Essentials is a clear and comprehensive foundational overview of the purpose and multifaceted role of the Human Resources function within an organization. Ms. Gilbert builds upon the history of the nature of work, pre and post-Industrial Revolution, building an important chronology that depicts how 'work' and 'workers' have evolved in response to shifting societal needs and how effectively managing human resources is a business imperative for organizational success and sustainability. Through a compelling integration of theoretical and conceptual content, relevant process models, and real-world practices and resources, Ms. Gilbert offers both a strategic and tactical resource for developing a sound knowledge base and skill set in human resource management that can be leveraged for more advanced deep-dive examination of each HR topic as well as applied in actual professional settings and contexts."

> **– Carrie A. Picardi, Ph.D. (Organizational Psychologist)**
> **Associate Professor of Management**
> **University of Bridgeport**

"The book on Human Resource Management Essentials provides strong functional knowledge of HRM and will enable students to clearly understand the purpose, practice and procedures attributed to HRM. The author has a comprehensive knowledge of the field and shares excellent real world examples. This book will be a desk reference both for the HRM major as well as for the business major with a different concentration, long after they graduate and embark upon their careers."

> **– Fernán R. Cepero**
> **MA, MS, PHR, SHRM-CP, Organizational &**
> **Global Leader Senior Human Resources Business Partner**
> **YMCA OF GREATER ROCHESTER - ASSOCIATION OFFICE**

What experts say about this book!

"This book gives a complete perspective of the entire gamut in Human Resources. On reading this book, you will get a comprehensive understanding of the Employee Lifecycle – right from hiring to exit from the organization. This textbook serves as a guide to understand the fundamentals on every aspect of Human Resources. Its principles can be applied while functioning as a human resource professional in any organization."

> – Rhea Doshi (M.SC Counselling Psychology)
> Manager Global Business Services - Learning & Development
> at BASF India Ltd

"Jaquina Gilbert's topical text on Human Resource Management provides a thoughtful introduction on the foundations to becoming a great HR leader. The content is as expansive as it is digestible. Gilbert does a great job establishing the business case for HR while providing tactile responses to the most sort out cases. I recommend this book to anyone considering a career in the field."

> – Anthony W. Caputo
> Vice President - Remesh
> Adjunct Professor - Seton Hall University

What experts say about this book!

"Jaquina Gilbert writes a simple and powerful guide to "Human Resources Management Essentials". She deftly has cut through the noise and provided an systematic overview of what modern HR leaders think of HRM systems in the 21st century. In an easy to read manner, she explains the essential components of an effective HRM strategy. The book is effective not only for HR students and leaders, but for novice non-HR practitioners who are involved in manpower planning and other HR decisions. I would highly recommend Jaquina Gilbert's book as an essential copy for emerging business leaders."

– Yogita Abichandani, Ph.D.
Associate Professor, HR & OB at Management Development Institute Murshidabad
Board Member - SECU, North Carolina | Co-Chairperson- Academy of HRD USA, INDIA SIG.
Chairperson- International Relations
Alumni - University of Georgia

"After a long time, it's good to have come across a book which gives detailed information on Human Resource Management. The author has covered all aspects of HRM in detail, right from the evolution of HRM to key roles, Legal aspects, Payroll, Compensation and Benefits, IT in HR, Health and Safety, etc. Each aspect has been looked at from a different perspective, keeping the current scenario in mind. This book will benefit both current HR professionals and future HR managers."

– Paras Panchamia
Manager - HR & Admin
Insight Business Machines Pvt. Ltd

What experts say about this book!

"This text on Human Resource Management Essentials is a solid read, and is a very good introduction to fundamental HR principles. Well-organized and written, the book includes easy-to-read and useful "how to" pieces and serves as a terrific resource for daily HR operators, leaders and managers."

          – **Paul W. Thurman, DBA**

          Professor of Management and Analytics

          Columbia University

"Human Resource Management Essentials is a basic, non-technical and easy read for anyone who wants general knowledge of the concepts of human resources. It is a great resource for small businesses and anyone who is currently in a non-HR role, but wants to understand the essentials of the field."

          – **Felicia D. Harris-Foster,**

          MBA, MS-HRM, CFE & Adjunct Faculty

Jaquina Gilbert has years of experience and knowledge that she has incorporated into the text, "Human Resource Management Essentials You Always Wanted to Know." Ms. Gilbert brings a wealth of expertise as she articulates general themes that stem from Human Resource Management (HRM). HRM is an essential discipline for scholars, employees, and employers to acknowledge as it sets a foundation for employer and employee relations.

Throughout this book, the author has brought forth her knowledge to bestow on others. Theories discussed throughout the book include Universalistic, Contingency, and Resource-Based. Soft and Hard Models led to the author's statement to entail, "The organization is more concerned with its growth while not being attentive to the work and welfare of the workers". This statement is an excellent point that brings up the need for and development of Human Resources Management at all levels of employees within a firm.

Human Resource Productivity introduces strategies to implement and increase employee productivity. Employees seek instant gratification for work performance, and employees who need remedial job training should be addressed early on as opposed to waiting for annual performance reviews. Presented in the text, are legalities discussed regarding the protection of the firm and employees. Discussed in the book is Organization development to walk through the planning concepts from the bottom up within the firm. Communication is key to HRM as it will set the tone of the work environment, which will affect both productivity and the firm's profits.

Conflict resolution is reality and must not be overlooked, to avoid conflicts, is it wise for the employer to offer conflict resolution groups to mediate against conflicts within departments and management. A hostile work environment leads to lower levels of productivity and bad morale among employees. The goal of the firm is to encourage issues to be addressed early as opposed to waiting until the problem escalates to Human Resources.

Payroll and compensation should be determined based on the firm's profits, which will dictate employee compensation. A firm must be aware of variable costs, which are costs that fluctuate from month-to-month as opposed to fixed costs that do not vary from month-to-month. Typically, a firm will have fixed costs in the short run, but in the long run, the firm will face variable costs. According to the author, the following factors will determine employee compensation salary, wages, fiscal bonus, indirect commissions, promotion, tour, and non-fiscal gift.

Discussed in the text is an overview of IT application in Human Resource Management to include strengths and weaknesses. Since our economy is a virtual environment, the need for IT arises. As technology is evolving quickly, there is a need for a Human Resource Information System (HRIS) and Human Capital Management (HCM). Discussed in the text are HRM,

HRIS, HCM are comparison and contrast between the three concepts of HRIS, HMC, HRM.

Health and safety development are important because without the proper vices in place; a firm will experience low levels of employee production and possible regulatory noncompliant punishment. Identified in the text is the need for a safe and healthy work environment. Depending on the type of work performed by employees, the firm may require potential employees to take a physical to ensure the safety of the firm; and, most of all, the safety and well-being of the potential employees.

In closing, people's development leads to a higher level of productivity and employee satisfaction with their current employment. The importance of people's development includes employee self-growth, improved employer-employee relationship, timely production, and healthy competition among employees. Coaching and mentoring should be an on-going process that promotes personal growth, promotions and rewards, and personal development. When HRM is employed effectively, the firm and employees both win and a firm's profits will rise. It should be apparent that the goal of HRM is to establish an inviting work environment that is conducive to employee growth and safety. Now, let's get started!

– Audra Sherwood, Ph.D.

Professor at Grand Canyon University

SELF-LEARNING MANAGEMENT SERIES

TITLE	PAPERBACK* ISBN
ACCOUNTING, FINANCE & ECONOMICS	
COST ACCOUNTING AND MANAGEMENT ESSENTIALS	9781636511030
FINANCIAL ACCOUNTING ESSENTIALS	9781636510972
FINANCIAL MANAGEMENT ESSENTIALS	9781636511009
MACROECONOMICS ESSENTIALS	9781636511818
MICROECONOMICS ESSENTIALS	9781636511153
PERSONAL FINANCE ESSENTIALS	9781636511849
ENTREPRENEURSHIP & STRATEGY	
BUSINESS PLAN ESSENTIALS	9781636511214
BUSINESS STRATEGY ESSENTIALS	9781949395778
ENTREPRENEURSHIP ESSENTIALS	9781636511603
GENERAL MANAGEMENT	
BUSINESS LAW ESSENTIALS	9781636511702
DECISION MAKING ESSENTIALS	9781636510026
LEADERSHIP ESSENTIALS	9781636510316
PRINCIPLES OF MANAGEMENT ESSENTIALS	9781636511542
TIME MANAGEMENT ESSENTIALS	9781636511665

*Also available in Hardback & Ebook formats

SELF-LEARNING MANAGEMENT SERIES

TITLE	PAPERBACK* ISBN
HUMAN RESOURCE MANAGEMENT	
DIVERSITY IN THE WORKPLACE ESSENTIALS	9781636511122
HR ANALYTICS ESSENTIALS	9781636510347
HUMAN RESOURCE MANAGEMENT ESSENTIALS	9781949395839
ORGANIZATIONAL BEHAVIOR ESSENTIALS	9781636510378
ORGANIZATIONAL DEVELOPMENT ESSENTIALS	9781636511481

MARKETING & SALES MANAGEMENT	
DIGITAL MARKETING ESSENTIALS	9781949395747
MARKETING MANAGEMENT ESSENTIALS	9781636511788
SALES MANAGEMENT ESSENTIALS	9781636510743
SERVICES MARKETING ESSENTIALS	9781636511733

OPERATIONS & PROJECT MANAGEMENT	
AGILE ESSENTIALS	9781636510057
OPERATIONS & SUPPLY CHAIN MANAGEMENT ESSENTIALS	9781949395242
PROJECT MANAGEMENT ESSENTIALS	9781636510712
STAKEHOLDER ENGAGEMENT ESSENTIALS	9781636511511

*Also available in Hardback & Ebook formats

About the Author

Jaquina Gilbert has over 20 years of Human Resources experience in multiple disciplines and holds both SHRM and PHR certifications. She authored three books and has written HR-related content for business owners, authors, and professionals in various industries. Jaquina received a BBA in Human Resources Management and Organizational Behavior from the University of North Texas in Denton, and an MS in Human Resource Training and Development from Amberton University.

This page is intentionally left blank

Table of Contents

10 People Development 201

Chapter 1

The Concept Of Human Resource Management

Chapter one introduces Human Resource Management (HRM) as both a term that defines a management function and an operating department within an organization. The chapter outlines the progressive existence of HRM and recounts various perspectives, theories, and approaches to the concept. The purpose is to ensure the reader's understanding of the definition, evolutionary progress, opposing viewpoints, basic functions, and challenges of Human Resource Management.

Key learning objectives should include the reader's understanding of the following:

- The nature and concerns of HRM

- How Human Resource Management evolved to what it is today

- The theories governing the principles of Human Resource Management

- The various approaches and their effect on the concept of Human Resource Management

- Why Human Resource Management is necessary but not compulsory

- Responsibilities and challenges for a human resource manager

Most modern organizations are victims of issues such as regulatory compliance, employee-underperformance, relatively low outputs, and many more. As a result, such organizations either become stagnant or witness a rapid decline in productivity. This decline fosters the purpose for which Human Resource Management (HRM) has either already been or should be established. Human Resource Management is consequently tasked with planning strategies to solve these problems.

Human Resource Management is a description of formalities and established patterns targeted at creating problem-solving strategies for the progress of an organization. It is a simple scheme that employs policies, practices, and systems to close any unpromising gaps between the company, management, and staff. These impending gaps could be both abstract and concrete. However, the objective of HRM is to identify the gap(s) and implement the strategies that best impede the discord between the primary constituents of its purpose.

HRM policies, practices, and systems are developed and implemented with a focus on three primary components:

- Company/Organization

- Management

- Staff/Employees

Figure 1.1

Extensively, the company includes commodified resources (i.e., an organizational commodity) for productivity. For many companies, one of the most abundant resources is humans. Thus, human resources become an essential element for productivity and subsequent organizational performance. Organizations that seek to effectively address regulatory compliance issues, employee-underperformance, low outputs, and other pain points, must first safeguard its vital resource—its employees.

Employer-employee relationships can be complicated. Because the relationship introduces both abstract and concrete interaction such as sharing ideas, behavior, emotion, human capital, tangible work products, attitudes, performance, and more, there is a delicate means by which organizations must address protecting the relationships. Human Resource Management attempts to protect the relationship that fuels the human productivity element that contributes to the organization's success. This protection is best served by developing and implementing appropriate strategies to address issues that compromise the relationship between employees, management, and the company. Many organizations establish an individual business division or department referred to as Human Resource Management to be the developer, keeper, and enforcer of these problem-solving strategies.

Human Resource Management

The Human Resource Management division of an establishment is often tasked with duties pointing towards the general development of employees. This stems from interviews, analysis of an organizational stance – financial and proprietary, imparting excellent and yielding knowledge on employees, work discipline, curbing harassing and intimidating acts among staff in the company, and most importantly, holding and preserving the industrial and progressive relationship of an organization. Later in the text, we will explore commonly adopted and accepted general functions of HRM.

Staggering and various reports suggest the correct or appropriate human resource personnel to employee ratios. Leading consultants, SHRM (Society for Human Resource Management), business bloggers, and others have all shared what they deem to be best practices or the most common and effective strategies for when to employ HR personnel. On average, most reports and information suggest that a human resources professional should be hired when a company has approximately 40 employees. Above all, it is important to know that with the absence of this vital authority in any modern organization, there will be a series of challenges that affect the entire facets of the company. In essence, setbacks such as poor staffing, strained staff relationships, poor employer-employee connection, and various other hindrances would be everyday happenings. The key is to seek a human resource professional early enough in the process to avoid mishaps tied to compliance, law, recruitment, performance, development, retention, and separation.

1.1 Evolution of Human Resource Management

The term Human Resource Management stretches back to the ancient medieval period. However, recent studies suggest that the concept of Human Resource Management dates back to the beginning of time. Although the concept of human resources is as old as time, there is no explicit early acknowledgment of the Human Resource Management term. Further, the degree of an employer-employee relationship was more or less abysmal, which is why the concept is not so connected with the early days.

In the 1920s, new official posts were employed that promoted the growth of Human Resources. One such is the Labor Manager or Employment Manager post, which came on board as a check on the general buildup of an industry with a particular focus on labor and employees. This was mostly applicable in factories with high productivity for ease of production and production check/management. In turn, this triggered an exceptional boost in productivity at the expense of mere encouragement of employees, sometimes for a competitive advantage over other factories.

Human Resource Management moved to a fuller usage in the 1980s. However, it still surfaced in a time that failed to grasp the concept of the employer-employee relationship, which we often find present in modern-day establishments. Furthermore, it is believed to have attained its near-modern head-start from women's desire for a secure ground for themselves and their children. Beyond this, the focus for the concept was also on the vitality of better outputs in the industries.

A Historical Perspective

Human Resource Management as a term and as a field of study did not just come to be. It passed through several phases and labor divisions to forge its prominence within organizations. Practically, the medieval period saw the rise of Human Resource Management and its procession from an era limited to agriculture to industrialization and on to post-industrialization.

Pre-Industrial Revolution

As the name implies, this revolution encompassed a limited occupation in society. The primary occupation was agriculture, accompanied by handicrafts. The idea of industrialization was lacking, and as such, the use of mostly natural resources in a natural way owned the period.

To make simple the idea, here are the three main categories notable in three aspects – slavery, serfdom, and contracted labor.

- **Human Resource Management and Slavery**   The use of humans as workforce commenced on the mounds of slavery. The source of labor was majorly slaves purchased by masters to work on farms. The masters were often less concerned or not concerned with any aspects of staffing, including wellbeing, health, and working hours. On this ground, masters were unable to filter unproductive workers from the field. Instead, unable slaves were terribly dealt with and compelled to work under difficult and sometimes impossible conditions. However, there stood a closeness between the master and the slave. A loyal slave would often get a reward of some sort or get sold out to the better working ground. Eventually, some workers would depart and establish their own industries while some others remained with their masters.

- **Human Resource Management and Serfdom**
  Serfs were bound to the land and owned by feudal lords. Since the era was mainly feudal, the responsibility of serfs started and ended on agricultural grounds. Serfs enjoyed some sorts of treats from the feudal lords who often rewarded them. The reward could be in money or any valuable material thing.

- **Human Resource Management and Contracted Labor**
  As time evolved, human resources changed, and this altered the overall conception of labor. The days began to witness indentured or contracted labor who enjoyed most of the liberty over slaves and serfs. Masters tended to respect

the laborers during this time, and it was largely due to the contracted nature of the dealing. The masters, on seeing hardworking laborers, intended to keep them for longer periods through extended contracts or for a lifetime. To achieve this, masters introduced several work benefits, incentives, and some positive motivational influence for workers to remain happy and extend contracts.

Industrial Revolution (1750 - 1850)

The industrial revolution marked the end of the shift from agriculture to full-time industrialization. Communication was more prominent during this era than it had been in the past, and this bolstered the continuous growth of human resource acknowledgment. A salaried scale system for labor and a more passionate approach towards the treatment of workers in available industries emerged. The revolution was witnessed worldwide, and this caused unrest among the majority of workers. They needed to find practical ways to conquer the brewing situations that threatened their way of life.

Workers' hours were complemented with low wages. To address the concern, the institution of labor unions notably sprung up around 1790, and this provided more authoritativeness for industry workers. Personnel management divisions upped their game to a more skillful pattern of handling the situations that concerned public affairs.

Robert Owen is regarded as the father of personnel management. He is noted to have brought about the idea of reforming working hours for employees. In his company, Lanark Cotton Mills, he introduced an eight-hour work schedule, which is now commonly practiced by most establishments worldwide.

His idea was all in a bid to motivate workers into yielding better results for a competitive advantage over others. Alongside Charles Babbage, Robert Owen resorted to the notion that housing healthy workers would result in a perfect job.

Post Industrial Revolution (1850)

During this time, Frederick Taylor's principle of scientific management emerged as he continued to improve upon industrial efficiencies and became known as one of the first management consultants. Taylor focused on managing simple tasks to improve productivity. He believed that approaching the work from a more scientific methodology would increase production and alleviate the responsibility that was being placed only on the workers. The workers had been tasked with trying to figure out how to get an incentive or initiative for their productivity.

George Elton Mayo is regarded as the father of Human Resource Management. Elton Mayo, alongside Fritz Roethlisberger, observed the findings of the Hawthorne Effect, which argues for the need to have productive workers and excellent working conditions. This transformed the idea of increased human resource productivity to efficiency for a more attractive yield.

With the acclivity of the period frequented by scholarly approaches, the nature of Human Resource Management propagated with swiftness to a more modern structure. The concept of Human Resource Management now promotes industries' need to be attentive to the welfare of workers. It has further aided establishments to employ efficiency rather than the unskilled workforce. Despite the employment of skilled workers, Human Resource Management also encourages the need to train the workers to become more competent. Reciprocally, the industry would witness more productive financial growth.

1.2 Theories of Human Resource Management

Universalistic Theory

The universalistic theory of Human Resource Management is founded on the idea of best practice and high performances of work practices. It argues that the performance of the industry mainly has to do with the practices of available human resources. This suggests that a defective human resource would have a negative effect on the entire organization.

Moreover, universalists hold that whatever practice is good enough is being practiced worldwide. Organizations follow what works for the other organization in an attempt to maintain a durable, working, and productive atmosphere. Also, the success of a production industry is scaled by its financial performance. Therefore, the performance of such a company is determined by the practices of the workers or human resources. The vision of this theory is to develop a method that could be commonly practiced by concerned organizations worldwide to create a balancing working system that works for all.

Contingency Theory

The contingency theory is the complete opposite of the universalist theory of Human Resource Management. This theory argues that there can be no similar practice worldwide. On this note, industries and organizations are supposed to strategize a format that agrees with their business environment. For example, McDonald's staff have a specific way of making deliveries as well as packing fast food for customers. If such practice is transferred to an establishment such as a bank, the entire methods would conflict and, in turn, pose threats to the day to day activities. This is why the theory or model opposes universality. A view that what works in company Y will not work effectively in company X.

Resource-Based Theory

The unique term used to describe this theory is 'learning.' The resource-based theory argues that the knowledgeability of a worker would certainly contribute largely to the productivity of a company. An organization would gain more significantly by training its staff to become more skilled in their class. Once skilled, the worker would find it easier to cope with the demands of such an organization, and this would encourage high productivity within short periods.

Since human resources determine the growth and creation of a competitive sphere, it would be unhealthy for the staff to remain unknowledgeable for too long. Thus, staff or workers must be trained immediately and not allowed to wait until they adapt.

Figure 1.2

Hard	Soft
• Stricter control of the environment by management. • Organization is more concerned with its growth while not being attentive to the worker welfare. • Company's management style is rigid.	• Employees are a vital means of a company's competitive advantage. • The company is supposed to hold high, the integrity of its workers. • Recognizes human resources as critical to the successful growth.

Soft Model

The soft model or theory holds that the environment determines an employee's productivity. The position of Legge agrees that employees are a vital means of a company's competitive advantage. This is realized through the utmost commitment and flexibility and is often very valuable. Such an environment must be conducive and tributary. Here, the company is supposed to hold high, the integrity of its workers.

Workers are encouraged to busy themselves collectively for yielding organizational progress. Several scholars view it as a strategic approach for any company to convince its workforce into giving their all and being self-disciplined with their activities.

The soft theory also conceives and recognizes human resources as critical to the successful growth of an organization. The success of an establishment becomes a reality once there is a show of determination, commitment, persistence, and skillfulness, often acquired through training from the managers of the company. Such occasions would as well make possible the replacement of workers with another skilled worker in no time.

Hard Model

Unlike the soft model of Human Resource Management, the hard model is a traditional view of Human Resource Management with pressure from the side of management. This theory contends that liberating workers with excess immunity and freedom would result in low productivity and laziness. This model opposes the soft model in instances of worker liberty. There is stricter control of the environment by management, and it, in turn, strains the working atmosphere.

The organization is more concerned with its growth while not being attentive to the work welfare of the workers. Moreover, there is an absence of skill as well as lacking teamwork since skill is devalued. As a result, competence is determined and forced by the company. The company's management style remains rigid and could often be unyielding or not yielding enough.

1.3 Approaches to Human Resource Management

Human Resource Management features several approaches. Each of the approaches embodies its own unique viewpoint, which is very well disputable.

Some of the approaches to Human Resource Management are
highlighted here:

Management Approach

The focal point of this approach is simply management. This
looks at the managerial aspect of an organization and the workers
therein. It also involves the overall outlook and supervision of
the activities that ascertain the productivity of an organization.
Essentially, the management approach convolves the idea of staff
supervision, productivity check, as well as the welfare of the
company at all levels.

Strategic Approach

The Strategic Human Resource Management approach entails
the yield-ability of employees. The focus of this approach is
fixated at employees' problem-solving abilities and the ability to
rise to the occasion. This approach notably commences directly
from interviews. It is interview-focal as it looks to examine the
worth of potential or actual employees and what they can offer
to the collective productivity and growth of the organization. It is
basically what employees have to offer. In cases where a company
subscribes to the contingency theory, such a company would have
to drill such an employee to adapt despite being unfit.

Commodity Approach

This is more or less regarded as a traditional approach since
it is only interested in the production stance of a company. The
approach involves commodifying employees and could well do
away with such employees once the goal is attained. Sometimes,

such employees could be retained, but the sense here is that the company arbitrates what happens and at any moment. This agrees with the hard model of Human Resource Management, which is organization-concerned.

System Approach

Human Resource Management is a concept that comprises components to function. The components include all things, abstract, concrete, and humanly that contribute to the positive or negative yields of a company.

Human Resource Approach

Human resources possess the productive prowess to bolster up or down the position of a company. Because human resources create a competitive advantage, they must be regarded and even rewarded. This approach of Human Resource Management coincides with the soft theory, which argues human resources as essential for organizational growth. As John F. Kennedy once said, *"Our progress as a nation can be no swifter than our progress in education. The human mind is our fundamental resource."*

Proactive and Reactive Approach

A proactive management team saves organizations tons of losses and setbacks in productivity and gains. When an organization adopts a proactive approach, the chances are that there will be more effective decisions for the betterment of such an organization.

On the other hand, when an organization adopts a reactive approach, the chances of a steady decline becomes inevitable.

The reaction could be to address staffing problems, production problems, managerial problems, and more. Approaching organizational impediments continuously with a reactive formality would eventually lead to a breakdown of a part of the organization or the organization in entirety.

1.4 Basic Functions of Human Resource Management

Edwin Flippo (2007) posits that Human Resource Management is the *"planning, organizing, directing, controlling or procurement, development, compensation, integration, maintenance and separation of human resources to the end that individual, organizational, and social objectives are accomplished."*

According to Flippo's definition of Human Resource Management, it is clear that this concept refers mainly to the supervisory and managerial forms of an organization.

Additionally, other leading minds in the HR realm have suggested primary functions of human resources management. These primary functions are typically broken down into:

- Managerial functions
- Operative functions

The managerial functions are comprised of:

- Planning

- Staffing

- Organizing

- Directing

- Controlling

The operative functions are more widely suggested as various individuals have contributed to their idea of a comprehensive list. Most familiar, the operative functions are characterized as:

- Recruitment or hiring

- Job analysis and design

- Performance appraisal

- Training and development

- Compensation

- Wage and salary administration

- Benefits administration

- Employee health and welfare

- Maintenance and retention

- Labor and employee relations

- Research

- Legal compliance

- Records management

Figure 1.3

Human Resource Management

Recruitment of Skilled Employees

It is ideal for maintaining an intelligent and skillful workforce by employing the best talent to complement the roles, the culture and the vision of the company. Human Resource Management is responsible for the intake of persons they perceive would be of a great addition and purpose to the company. Recruitment of otherwise unfit persons would mean a decline in the productivity and competitive prowess of the organization.

Directing

A company's human resources or workers may, at some point, not know what or what not to do. Human Resource Management then attempts to set objectives and put the human resources on a course to success. Without that, productive activities might be approaching the wrong course.

The Utility of Available Resources

Both human and nonhuman resources are necessary to yield the best efficiency and progress for an organization. The idea of the establishment of Human Resource Management then bolsters the chances of being able to utilize what is available. This could involve apportioning duties to the available workforce/nonhuman resource to achieve a goal or maintain a relatively strong competitive advantage.

Ensuring a Healthy Employer-Employee Relationship

Human Resource Management ensures fluidity in the dealings between employers and employees. John Kennedy also said, *"The human mind is our fundamental resource."* This suggests that in a situation where there is a tangled relationship between an employer and the employee, the affairs of the business would be affected. In this case, the concept of Human Resource Management brings about a balanced relationship between employers and employees.

Training and Development of Employees

For better company performance, workers must be qualified, skilled, and trained. Either the worker is allowed to adapt to the system or is trained to develop at a faster pace. Allowing a worker to adapt naturally would cost time and generate ineffective yields. However, training such individuals would aid the organization significantly.

1.5 The Human Resource Manager

Human Resource Management comprises a human member or members. Human resource managers are responsible for the supervision, controlling, procurement, and management of human resources. They are the link between employers and employees, and they often validate decisions pertaining to the human resourcefulness of an organization.

The human resource manager position is a professional type. It requires the psychological ability to handle situations proactively and reactively. Decisions are incredibly impactful and can either leave a blemish or create a sound, consistent practice for the company. Moreover, some of the conventional qualities of human resource managers include oratorical prowess, an actively thinking mind, the ability to dissolve pressure, excelled communication skills, and, most importantly, excellent leadership skills. All of these are put together for the description of human resource managers.

Some Responsibilities of the Human Resource Manager

Human resource managers are tasked with hefty responsibilities, especially that they act as a decisive measure for the productivity of a company. However, a competent and skilled human resource manager should possess at least the following attributes and be able to perform the following functions:

- The ability to plan, organize, manage, carry along, and set employees on the same course

- Setting up procedures that will permeate an instant or later yield to the organization's productive ability

- Developing fresh ideas targeted at the collective growth of the organization as well as the employees

- Reviewing job descriptions and functions before recruitment publications

- Recruiting skilled employees to boost productivity

- Working with the human resource team to ensure a steady competitive position in an organization

- Advocating for the introduction of policies capable of affecting the organizational structure of a company positively

- Overseeing the activities of employees and allocating the fitting duty to employees

- Creating a well-disposed link between employees and the employer

- Suggesting a change or changes in a particular or overall structure or system of operation for betterment

- Reviewing salaries and recommending a new salary scale

- Creating a friendly work atmosphere and encouraging employees with their jobs

- Enforcing and maintaining legal compliance necessary to promote organizational growth

- Promoting and developing training and development opportunities for all levels within the organization

- Ensuring appropriate staffing levels to maintain a productive workflow

- Serving as a sounding-board for manager and employee questions relating to a safe, healthy, productive and suitable work environment and culture

Figure 1.4

Duties and Responsibilities of Human Resource Managers

Develop a thorough knowledge of corporate culture, plans and policies

Act as an internal change agent and consultant

Initiate change and act as an expert and facilitator

Actively involved in company's strategy formulation

Keep communication line open between the HRD function and individuals and groups both within and outside the organization

Identify and evolve HRD strategies in consonance with overall business strategy

Employee Recruitment and Selection

Employee Training and Performance Evaluation

Employee Compensation and Benefits

Employee Counseling

Planning for Staffing Needs

Team Building

1.6 Challenges Faced by Human Resource Management

Human Resource Management encounters problems that require mental strength to solve. It can be challenging having to deal with these situations because most of these challenges are unpredictable. Moreover, making certain decisions could very well aid or adversely damage the company. A human resource manager would not welcome wrong decisions, and this means occasionally having to work with and determine the probability of mishaps and issues.

Some of the challenges faced by Human Resource Management include:

Employer-Employee Relationship

Creating an affectionate closeness between the employer and employee is one of the problems that confront human resource managers. Sometimes, a human resource manager may have to defend and lean more toward the employee's behavior or perspective, even where the employee has shown low productivity. Such productivity could be due to the lack of or limited availability of nonhuman resources. Human resource managers may also have to protect employees who are subject to harsh, illegal, violent, or other undesirable working conditions. Sometimes the human resource manager is unaware of these circumstances, but it is always the best decision to alleviate the threats or uncomfortable situations and then to determine a solution to prevent future reoccurrence.

It can be difficult to manage behaviors that invoke an individual's personality, upbringing, religious beliefs, emotions, and other non-tangible characteristics that define an employee's identity. These abstract components can often cause employers to be unable to ascertain an employee's expectations or desires. The human resource manager is tasked with helping to build a bridge between these intangible characteristics and leveraging them to solidify a strong and reliable employer-employee relationship that benefits both parties. It is challenging because the human resource manager would attempt to justify both parties while keeping impartial in the process. In cases where an employer is highhanded, it affects the organization as workers would lose the appropriate encouragement. It is then the human resource manager's place to compensate for the situation and ignite that 'readiness to work' factor in employees.

Productivity

Some elements of an organization's overall productivity are attributed to the effectiveness of a human resource manager. Human resource managers must make constant decisions and considerable suggestions to prevent the company from backsliding at a quicker or slower pace. This may include staffing recommendations, policy suggestions, or implementing specific systems that could assist with increasing productivity.

The performance of a company could rest on the shoulders of a human resource person, and both failure and a win would draw all eyes to inspect the impactful role.

Accommodating Changes

Once in a while, establishments witness great innovation. They are often technological innovations and advancement as the world is growing at a quicker pace. This type of rapid growth can pose a bit of strategizing difficulty as teams try to adapt to trends quickly. Without adapting and adapting well, human resource managers may be looked upon as lacking brilliance or vitality. It is imperative that human resource managers or teams are prepared to lead the way in change management, and that they are fully capable of developing effective strategies to bring all other teams and individuals onboard.

Dealing with Labor Unions

When employees feel that their working conditions, environment, or treatment are unjust, they may choose to act collectively and form or join a labor union. Unions then become a resource for those employees to have a collective voice that will represent or speak on their behalf against the employer. It is designed to represent the members' interests and to help resolve issues that arise between the employee and employer.

Not all organizations have unionized labor or a unionized workforce. In companies that have a workforce that is represented by a union, there are very specific processes and rules for addressing concerns. In general, there are occasions when a company's decision conflicts with employees' demands. The employee may seek counsel or guidance from their union representative to help navigate the conversation with the employer. The human resource person is most commonly involved and would have to handle the situation using extreme communication, leadership, listening, and negotiation and mediation skills. These talents are important to ensure professionalism in the process and to guarantee better results for resolution. Human resource managers should approach situations with high intelligence, making sure they fully grasp the perspective of the employee and the impact of the union representation. Human resource managers should evade saying or making decisions that could be costly to the organization both in the financial and legal realm.

Figure 1.5

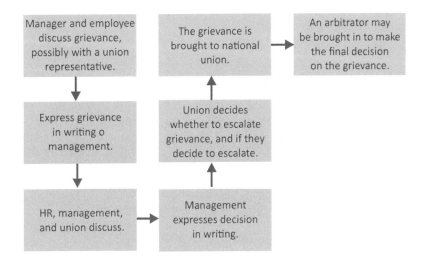

Selecting the Best Employees

Selecting the best individual for the job is often challenging. Where many persons are applying with almost similar qualifications and experiences, it becomes difficult to determine who is a better fit for the company. In cases such as this, human resource persons employ a series of roadmaps to help determine the course of action. It does not happen seamlessly, but with diligent recruiting and assessment efforts, selecting the best-fit individual for the position can work out just fine. The roadmap begins with recruitment efforts and ends with the placement of the best-qualified individual to perform the job.

Developing a Swift Workflow and Conducive Work Environment

It is necessary to create an atmosphere that is conducive enough for employees to feel safe, productive, and welcome. When the working environment is interactive and swift-going, there is a presence of commitment. As such, most employees would practice a greater extent of self-discipline in a bid to satisfy the company wholly. However, this is a concept that the hard model opposes as it believes that such an atmosphere promotes unyielding results and encourages laziness among employees.

Chapter Summary

◆ Human Resource Management (HRM) is both a term that defines a management function and an operating department within an organization.

◆ HRM, as a practice, has existed from the Medieval period through the Renaissance period to the modern period.

◆ The evolution of HRM spans a historic preindustrial, industrial, and post-industrial time.

◆ An organization must adopt a theoretical approach as it helps such a company to identify its goals easily.

◆ There are several approaches to HRM, which include: Management, Strategic, Commodity, System, Human Resource, and Proactive and Reactive approaches. A company may not adopt all of these approaches but must identify a type that aids in attaining a goal.

◆ HRM is necessary for a company to maintain a competitive advantage.

◆ A human resource person has various responsibilities and is a vital personality in any organization seeking to make progress and maintain balance.

◆ There primary functions of HRM are typically characterized by managerial functions and operative functions.

Quiz 1

1. Human Resource Management uses all of the following, except _____ to create problem-solving strategies that help the progressiveness of the company, management, and employees within the organization.

   a. systems

   b. productivity

   c. practices

   d. policies

2. Dan is the CEO of a large retail chain. His best friend, John, is a VP of a large successful hotel empire. Dan and John discussed ways to make their employees more productive so that they could increase bottom-line profits. Dan ultimately adopted all of the practices and processes that John has put in place at his company. Dan's view of employee's productivity likely embraces the:

   a. Hard Model

   b. Contingency Theory

   c. Resource-Based Theory

   d. Universalistic Theory

3. **An approach, stemming from interviews, that is primarily concerned about employee's problem-solving abilities and what an employee can offer toward the growth of a company is a(n):**

   a. Commodity Approach

   b. Management Approach

   c. Strategic Approach

   d. Human Resource Approach

4. **Which is not a recognized managerial function of HRM?**

   a. Staffing

   b. Organizing

   c. Directing

   d. Training

   e. Controlling

5. **Select the statement that is False.**

    a. Under the Resource-Based Theory, a view that works in company Y will not work effectively in company X.

    b. Human Resource Managers sometimes have to defend employee's behavior even when the employee has been a low performer, showing low-productivity.

    c. Human Resource Managers have to make constant decisions and many suggestions

    d. Most HR challenges are unpredictable, but proper planning, sound decision making, and implementing problem-solving strategies can help to face the challenge.

Solutions to the above questions can be downloaded from
the **Online Resources** *section of this book on*
www.vibrantpublishers.com

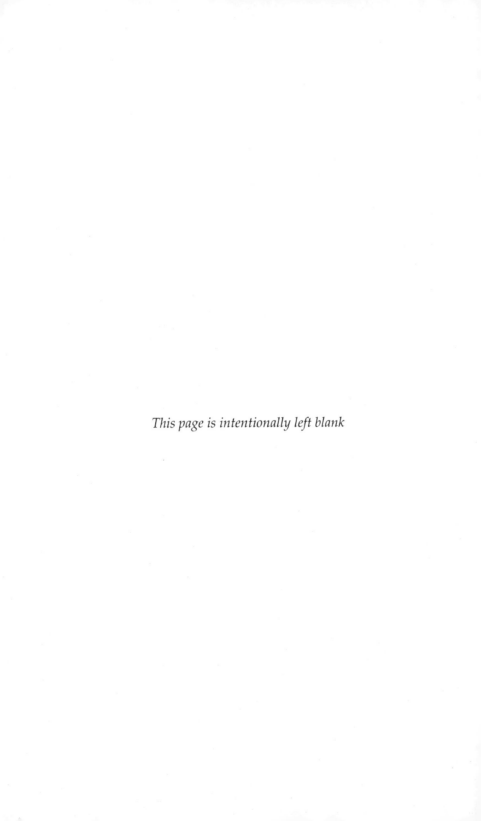
This page is intentionally left blank

Chapter 2

Performance Management Strategies

This chapter explains performance management and highlights seven implementation strategies. Human Resource professionals should integrate these strategies for increased effectiveness within any organization. The chapter expounds performance management by identifying the purpose of the various strategies, effective methodology, and a general cycle for measuring performance.

Readers should be able to assess the following upon completing the chapter:

- The potential effectiveness of integrating the seven performance management strategies

- What makes performance management strategies relevant and the need to be strategic

- How a Human Resource person can structure strategies to arrive at a desired goal

- The purpose behind the performance management cycle and how it shapes the expectations of a company

Getting the working atmosphere to a spark that lures commitment and boosts employees' performance remains the fundamental objective when motoring human resources. Performance relies on how collectively committed employees are as a team or individually to boost productivity. Performance management is the organization's way of making sure that the individual activities and outputs of each employee contributes to the organization's overall goals. A human resource person or team would charge towards merit as a goal. For such a result, performance must be good. No matter an organization's theoretical approach in the daily business, what matters, in the end, is the collective performance leading to productivity.

Human Resource Management inclined organizations rely solely on managing their workforce or humans. This immediately correlates to the various performance management strategies utilized within certain establishments to attain set goals. The idea is to both motivate employees and to enact policies that agree with both the employee morals and the principles of the law.

There are no traditionally accepted formalities on the question of performance management strategies. However, several collections of systemic plan-to-action based on tests have been introduced over time.

Here are seven strategic actions to apply for enhanced and flawless human resources performance management:

Establish and Encourage Transparency

Moore (1995) suggests that transparency is a key part of the process. Public managers are expected to continually inform and educate their stakeholders, going beyond their legal obligations for information disclosure. It thus helps the managerial system where there is the presence of transparency. HR managers are expected to communicate the need for transparency to the board (or upper executive leadership), where applicable, and show by example. Just as in Moore's thought, go beyond obligations to inform the stakeholders for enhanced productivity.

Design a Crystal-Clear Model

It is pivotal to employ a vivid human resource development managerial model. Where the outlook is vague, it becomes tough for other managers and sub managers of the organization to cope. Bear in mind that a crystal-clear model is a key aspect of the entire process of human resource development. Moreover, despite being crystal-clear, emphasize, and restate the envisioned achievement. Go on and create an avenue where employees and managers can ask and re-ask questions concerning the modeling. Whatever the model at hand, it must be comprehensible to even the least of the categories of employees.

Encourage Frequent Evaluation

Encouraging employees to evaluate their activities is a brilliant performance management strategy. This provides room for such an employee to discover whether or not they are performing in the system. This strategy encourages an employee and even managers to stay focused and disciplined in a bid to match up with the required work productivity. The underlying idea is that no staff wishes to be the least rated in any establishment.

Reward Excellence, Commitment, and Discipline

Scholars like Coff and Kryscynski have consistently emphasized the importance of reward. Recent studies further claim that reward, as a practiced system in any organization, is very effective in the growth of the organization. In line with this, Alpkan et al. (2010) hold that *"… continuing rewards system can encourage the entrepreneurs to consistently build new ideas and foster creativity as well as commitment towards innovation."* Rewarding hard work is a basic performance management strategy that works in any organization that is pursuing higher outputs.

Keep Communication Alive

An article by Mark Amele (TrainingZone) states that communication is necessary because miscommunication can land in blunders that hit the growth of a company. This is the reason why it is sometimes not wise to practice the hard model of Human Resource Management due to its rigidity. Communication must stay alive by frequently interacting with the employees. If possible, the objectives and accomplishments of each department should be communicated to others. You never know, a particular team might learn from the other team and then perform better by mending the flaws initially suffered by the other team in their operation.

Inform and Carry the Team Along

A sound performance management tactic is never to assume the team already knows what is going on. It is strategic to question the managerial team and request that they question the employees. There might be something about your new model that perplexes everyone who finds it challenging to communicate. When the best human resource suddenly experiences a decline in performance, it is often a result of 'thinking' that they know. This will as well result in having a worker who is off track and far away from the new model, continue to perform poorly unknowingly. This is often the case when there are innovations in a company that require adaptations. Keep the employers well-informed and ensure that every available individual stays on course. Some human resource persons make it a habit to draft a summary that regularly gives hints to employees about what is required of them. Consider doing the same, but be cautious not to overwhelm or to bombard employees with unwelcomed or unwarranted reminders.

Do Not Impose Unnecessarily

A 2019 study in the United States discovered that impositions in workplaces make jobs more difficult. To curb the difficulty and replace it with swiftness, it is advisable to make suggestions rather than impose immediately on employees. This is a key skill for human resource managers to employ. Learning to aid or assist without solely commanding a situation is imperative. Imposition in workplaces is said to be dictatorial and is classified as the traditional way of winning employees into remaining committed, dedicated, and perfect with their jobs. But let's be honest. No one wants to work under a dictator who only sees the value in their own opinions, processes, and direction.

2.1 Basics of Performance Management Strategies

The basics of performance management are not in any way absurd or difficult to grasp. The primary idea lies in being convincing enough to encourage the available human resources. Remember, the minds of the people are necessary for the growth of the business or organization. Thus, it would not be enchanting to shift aside the values of performance management.

Here are the fundamentals of performance management and the effects they have on the system:

Liberating Grouped Workers with Workflow

Performance management promotes a sort of workflow that is appealing to workers. This happens when a human resource person or department can ascertain who is and who is not perfect for a particular duty. With performance management strategies, it becomes relatively easy for an organization to define the role an individual's skills would best fit. When the role and the individual are strategically matched, managing the performance and workflow becomes more seamless. In essence, workers are liberated through their performance and workflow because they can operate in a comfort zone.

Hiring Suitable Personnel

Every organization needs the perfect talent and skills for the job. Mostly, the human resource department is tasked with the responsibility, and this means employing a highly skilled person for the job. The idea here lies in selection. Usually, human resource persons utilize specific company guides to make ease of the selection process, while other human resource persons prefer to utilize what an individual brings to the table. Well, these are all vibrant fundamental performance management strategies that could yield desired results. More often than not, the results usually meet expectations, and this can only happen with a properly designed benchmark.

Making the Work Environment Conducive

It is one of the many strategic features of performance management to create a conducive work environment. Productivity undoubtedly relies on performance, and performance relies on human resources. When the human mind is relaxed, there is bound to be increased yield, and this means commitments coupled with high output.

However, conduciveness should be accompanied by frequent and unexpected checks on the workforce. The hard model argues that work add-ons such as excess conduciveness promote laziness, and this results in low yield or productivity. It is, therefore, advisable to invent and employ strategies to check on the conduciveness permeated by an established performance management strategy.

Scrutinizing Employee Performance

It is fundamental for performance management strategies to help scrutinize the abilities and skills of an employee. The scrutiny does not automatically suggest a negative outcome or view of the performance. However, after such scrutiny, the human resource arm is supposed to reward, encourage, or discipline an employee. The performance management strategies undeniably help to pick out certain skilled individuals, collate, scrutinize, and conclude. The results may vary significantly. Sometimes the scrutiny reveals that an employee needs more training, deserves a reward, or is worthy of encouragement.

Keeping Employees Informed of Performance

This is a communication tactic that lets the employee know how highly or lowly impactful their performance has been. It is pertinent to either maintain productive performance levels or to address less than desirable performance levels. Keeping the employee informed of their progress and performance can be as simple as a brief statement or a lengthier conversation. Before reporting low performance to an employee, it is ideal to be sure that the cause of such low productivity has no connection with the management practices of the organization. It is one of the basics of performance management strategies that help the industry to keep healthy competition alive.

Seasoned Performance Review

Performance management strategies encourage seasoned reviews of an organization. It should be a norm to charge human resource persons with timely checks on the entire progress of the organization. This practice helps to sort and ascertain where a company suffers lapses. Performance management, in this regard, could be made highly successful. One such way is making copies of the organizational happenings and sharing information with workers in the form of reports, memos, or discussions at open meetings.

2.2 Objectives of Performance Management Strategies

The objective of any performance management strategy is to review and reward excellence. It is essential to make employee objectives correspond with those of the company. Employed individuals could work but remain unaligned with the objectives of the company. Failing to align the objectives could result in tremendous mishaps leading to declines in bottom-line figures, employee morale, and much more. By correctly aligning the objectives, individuals may exhibit corporate core values that impact creativity in the business and also bring about high productivity.

Moreover, performance management also aims at encouraging high skills and furthered intelligence. It sets up a cultured model that keeps the workforce on course without confusion or unclear expectations. Performance management strategy objectives also promote self-discipline, employee motivation, and a positive working atmosphere.

Here are some common goals of performance management strategies:

Clarity of Goals

The purpose of performance management strategies is to present a clear definition of company goals. This even helps a company to predict its future. Where the goals and objectives are absurd, it becomes near impossible to attain a level of success. Therefore, performance management is vital as it aims toward identifying a goal and keeping everyone on course to achieve it.

A Good Employer-Employee Relationship

Both employers and employees are necessary for production. A good performance management strategy is to develop goals that make it relatively easy to build a good working relationship between the employer and employees. The focus is not entirely on the relationship but takes it into consideration as not to strain the connection between the two. Doing so could hamper the company's overall objective.

Encouraging Individual Employee Growth

Proper performance management can bring excellence to fruition. There is bound to be growth when staff is encouraged frequently. In the same vein, it is crucial to identify the flaws that staff may have and to delicately bring them to the employee's attention, so that they do not erroneously believe their performance is the pillar of perfection. Some proponents of the hard model hold that encouragement would lead to the employee feeling too good for a task. On the other hand, the productivity level of such an employee might suffer a decline. However, proponents of the soft model hold that encouragement is one of the basic human resource managerial components. With regard to these arguments, contingent proponents hold that practicing soft or hard model approaches in an organization would depend on the type of organization.

Handy Transparency

In the words of Florini (2007), transparency is *"the release of information which is relevant for evaluating institutions."* This goes on to highlight that with transparency, evaluation is possible, and this is a vital objective of performance management in any organization. Performance management seeks to ensure that employees are aware of the organizational goals and that employee outputs are in alignment with achieving those goals. Without transparency to fully understand the purpose of the objectives and how each position impacts the achievement of such objectives, it may prove difficult to accomplish the desired success.

Swift and Excellent Skills Exploration

An organization requires decent human resource skills to function at its best. Without the presence of such skills, an organization would find it challenging to keep up with the sole demand of the venture. Quality performance management therefore targets excellent skills and employs various strategic formalities to uncover such skills. They may be uncovered from an individual who is already employed with the company or from among its list of promising recruits.

2.3 Purpose of Performance Management Strategies

Performance management, according to Armstrong and Baron (2004), is *"a process which contributes to the effective management of individuals and teams in order to achieve high levels of organizational performance."* This definition suggests that performance management is not just a one-individual thing but a collective organizational thing that includes the organization, human resource persons, and human resources or employees.

The general purpose of performance management is communicating a set goal and measuring how each individual contributes to achieving those set goals. In general, all concerned individuals must be trained and informed to achieve the goal. The purpose of performance management also extends to a more substantial part of the managerial system.

Here are the purposes of performance management strategies:

Bolstered Yield

Performance management strategies enhance high or improved yields. This results from the proper treatment of employees. Proper management of available human resources would promote high output and would require ensuring that employers remain happy.

Enhanced Communication

Communication is effective in any organization. Proper communication in an organization would establish a brilliant employer-employee relationship. The employer would be able to communicate difficulties directly or through the Human Resource Management team. This effort dramatically boosts productivity.

Employee Development

Performance management encourages individual development. It is what keeps a company at the edge of competitive advantage in its niche. Here, proper implementation of the performance management concept would assist in the productive growth of an organization. When an employee is well developed, handling responsibilities becomes easy and such an employee is able to connect with a team.

Other purposes of performance management include:

- Encouragement of commitments among managers and employees

- The presence of skilled workers

- Flexibility in teamwork

- Creating an enriched working atmosphere

- The encouragement of self-discipline among stakeholders of the company or establishment

2.4 Drafting Effective Performance Management Strategies

After outlining performance management strategies, the subsequent task is to facilitate such strategies. For this reason, human resource departments would proceed to draft something effective. The first thing to consider in the process is individual (employee) development and how to convince the employee to be committed. This aligns with John Lockett's (1992) opinion on performance management. Consider drafting effective performance management strategies that work universally in any practicing organization using Lockett's opinion.

Collect Performance Data

A proactive human resource person would consistently receive reports about employee performance data. It is the employer's place to request an audit of staff in the company. As a human resource person, inform the team of the need to collect seasoned work data, which would be used for a more detailed assessment of staff activities. This could be done daily, weekly, or monthly depending on the size of an organization. It will go on to ease the job load on the Human Resource Management team and ensure proactiveness in the Human Resource Management department.

Collate Performance Data

Collation is a stage of critical comparisons as well as the sequential and proper assembling of the collected records or data. It is ideal to share different department's data in an organization to make the collation task easier and near errorless.

Performance Appraisal

Performance appraisals can also be referred to as performance reviews or annual reviews. This is the next necessary draft to develop in order to establish effective performance management strategies. Performance appraisal is simply the formalities in the assessment of an employee's performance concerning the job allocated to him or her. The assessment involves how steady or consistent such an employee has been with the job and the effectiveness of his activities in the organization. An appraisal may either trigger rewarding a deserving employee or finding a solution and encouraging such an employee. It may also include assessing and addressing poor performance on the part of the employee and discussing resolutions.

Ask Questions

In cases where an appraisal reveals a lack of productivity in an employee's activities, it is ideal to talk things out. Do not judge the appraisal result; instead, find out why the employee delivered a less than desirable performance. There could be something the company should know, and this might be a burden on not just that staff but to others extensively. Questioning the situation would contribute largely to identifying problems, which could be a result of the managerial decisions or working atmosphere.

Solve Problems

After finding out the cause of underperformance, diligent managers or supervisors attempt to figure out a solution. For instance, when a company is in a transitional phase, it often requires a bit of time for employees to adapt to the new system. For such a cause, an employee may lag in the duties assigned. In cases where such an employee's reason(s) hint at a company-imposed workflow that often delegates employees to the wrong job, consider allowing such employees the liberty to suggest a more suitable workflow. For example, an employee who is excellent in coding might face difficulties in handling the promotional aspects of a company like advertising the brand using any social platform. Once confident of the cause of underperformance, report back to the Human Resource Management department. Make sure to conduct proper follow-up and devise a lasting solution.

Reward Excellence

High employee performance should be rewarded. The reward will encourage employees to perform even better in subsequent duties. Additionally, rewarding excellence establishes a stronger employer-employee relationship, infusing elements of loyalty, trust, and appreciation.

2.5 The Performance Management Cycle

Bill Gates commented on performance, saying, *"In business, the idea of measuring what you are doing, picking the measurements that count like customer satisfaction and performance... you thrive on that."* His comment about measurements, customer satisfaction, and performance incorporates three concepts that must act together for a positive result. The performance management cycle is seasonal or annual checks on employee performance. The system has regards for no category of employee and seeks to make amends and to drive every workforce unitedly towards a planned goal.

The primary target of this formality is to generate or discover strategies that work. This is why the strategy takes place mostly on an annual basis to rate employee performance and see what could be done to enhance performance. Ultimately, the idea of the performance management cycle keeps employees on course to deliver desired outputs. This is the case because employees generally fear receiving the least possible rating in any organization. The idea connects with the corporate core values of employees and attempts to match such values with the expectations of the organization. The cycle is coupled with advantages such as work effectiveness, job flexibility, staff commitment, and high competition among staff. It involves four stages, which include:

- Planning

- Monitoring

- Reviewing

- Rewarding

Figure 2.1

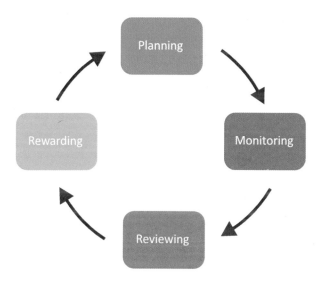

Planning

Planning is the first stage of the performance management cycle, and it deals with setting simple, achievable goals. Here, there could be minor but effective activities such as a description of the job at hand, outlining clear goals, and informing staff members of the expectations of the organization for the year. This phase should include understanding and incorporating the guiding principles of the organization. Further, management should identify performance objectives and strategies that have an employee focus.

While planning, let the plan agree with John Quincy Adams' statement that, *"If your actions inspire others to dream more, learn more, do more and become more, you are a leader."* Make plans that motivate an employee and that are flexible. Be part of the plans and try to carry every individual along.

In order to have a simpler performance management model, consider implementing the S-M-A-R-T technique. This is a technique for goal-setting. Goals or objectives should be:

- **S** – Specific – Be specific with the goal and ensure it is a clear goal for easy understanding in the organization.

- **M** – Measurable – All plans must be measurable and easy to comply with.

- **A** – Achievable – Do not plan on actions that are not easily achievable by the organization. Simply, be realistic with the plans.

- **R** – Relevant – All plans must be relevant and able to leave positive effects on organizational growth.

- **T** – Time-Bound – Do not make plans to borders away from achievable time.

One of the most essential processes in this phase is the last portion of it. Both the manager and employee (and sometimes HR) should agree and confirm the plans before implementing them. This ensures an understanding by all involved.

Monitoring

The second phase of the performance management cycle involves keeping tabs on the ongoing activities and businesses of the organization. Check up on the progress and employee performances in place towards achieving an organizational goal. Meet occasionally to discuss difficulties and proffer solutions. It is ideal to hear staff suggestions as they sometimes know what is best for the company since they are more involved in the production aspect. In this phase, a manager should provide ongoing coaching, counseling, mentoring, and guidance. They should also promote employee training and development opportunities in order to manage underperformance and disciplinary issues better.

Performance monitoring and development should be ongoing processes, that if encompassed with effective goal-setting, can build a bridge to employee success.

Reviewing

Review activities to identify how much of the goals have been met so far. In essence, here we determine the accountability effectiveness measures. Ideally, a review should result in taking measures to enhance the current situation. Further, it is essential to determine that the additional measures help to meet goals. Giving due attention to staff is critical. The staff could likely be declining as a result of specific new company policies, innovation, working environment, or poor employer-employee relationships. In order to uncover the cause, question such staff, and do not reprimand the staff in the process. Be encouraging to convince such staff to become more committed to the job. It is important to refer to previously developed plans to see if goals have been met. Determining rating results is important at this stage. At this stage, managers should provide feedback on the rating results and performance objectives. The keyword is feedback!

Rewarding

The fourth and final state of the performance management cycle is the rewards, remuneration, and recognition phase. This is an encouragement of an employee's performance for the season. Dale Carnegie (Leadership Training Guru) opines that *"People work for money but go extra mile for recognition, praise, and rewards."* Apart from money, workers also need recognition and deserving praises. What this means is that an employee who feels unrecognized will not remain committed. To encourage that desire to work more and dedicate more, a reward should be considered. Such rewards could come in many forms and may include gifts, promotion, increased salary, reduced work hours, and extended liberties. Rewards should not initially be tied to ratings or plans. Ratings should be used to evaluate performance. Meeting goals and objectives may ultimately be tied to monetary rewards such as bonuses or merit increases. Other rewards may include promotions, special recognition, or meeting requirements for certification.

This stage is also characterized by implementing performance improvement initiatives as or if necessary. If the employee did not meet desired goals and objectives, they should not necessarily be rewarded, but should also receive the appropriate follow-up to 'reward' their performance. This is sometimes done with performance improvement plans.

Here is a general or suggested performance management timeline:

Figure 2.2

Create Performance Plan

- Meet with New Hire to review job description, expectations and to develop a performance plan

TIMELINE - Within two (2) weeks of hire

Probationary or Periodic Feedback

- Provide periodic feedback on performance, Utilize notes, discussions and meetings to document on templates

TIMELINE - At two (2) months At four (4) months

Mid-Year Review

- Provide formal, substantive feedback on the employee's performance. Do not associate remuneration or rewards

TIMELINE - At six (6) months

End of Year Review

- Provide formal, substantive feedback on the employee's performance. Do not associate remuneration or rewards

TIMELINE - At one (1) year

Rewards/ Performance Improvement

- Performance Improvement as/if necessary via template and formal documentation
- Rewards/recognition as possible
- Remuneration as defined or allowable by budget

TIMELINE - Within three (3) months of final rating

Chapter Summary

◆ Performance management strategies are a vital aspect of HRM.

◆ For every well-structured strategy, a positive and rewarding result would be achieved.

◆ Effective performance management strategies should be drafted using a methodology that includes the collection of data, collation of performance data, performance appraisal, asking questions, solving problems and rewarding excellence.

◆ A proper performance management cycle comprises four stages including, planning, monitoring, reviewing, and rewarding. Moreover, the planning phase is best executed using the S-M-A-R-T technique for goal-setting.

Quiz 2

1. The Performance Management Cycle stages include:

   a. monitoring, goal setting, rewarding, legal compliance

   b. performance appraisal, monitoring, transparency, rewarding

   c. practices, performance appraisal, monitoring, evaluation

   d. rewarding, monitoring, planning, reviewing

2. **Jan is the HR Manager for Company X. One of the managers in the company, Daryl, asked Jan about the performance management process. Daryl mentioned that he would like to implement a training or developmental opportunity for his team before he provides a final assessment for one of his employees. Jan advised him that although his thoughts are commendable, they are approaching the last week of the evaluation period. She advised him that training can be initiated at any time, but that it fits more appropriately into the _____ phase of the performance management cycle.**

   a. Planning

   b. Training

   c. Rewarding

   d. Monitoring

3. **Placing an employee on a performance improvement plan (PIP) should occur in the _____ stage of the performance management cycle?**

   a. Evaluation

   b. Planning

   c. Rewarding

   d. Monitoring

4. **Which definition of performance management is most accurate?**

   a. It is how the company communicates its goals and subsequently makes sure the individual activities and outputs of each employee contribute to the organization's overall vision and set goals.

   b. It is designed to motivate employees.

   c. It is necessary to review and reward excellence.

   d. It is the encouragement of self-discipline among stakeholders of the company or establishment

   e. It is characterized by the acronym SMART.

5. **Select the statement that is True.**

   a. The performance management cycle is characterized by the five stages—using an acronym known as SMART.

   b. Information should be shared with employees that advise of the organizational happenings. Sharing information can be in the form of memos, reports, and at meetings.

   c. It is important for HR persons to take a direct stance with employees to ensure their compliance and commitment to the organization. Therefore, HR should curb suggestions and impose strict demands at all times.

   d. Performance management tries to distract the workforce by providing unclear expectations and difficult objectives for employees to prove their skills competencies.

Solutions to the above questions can be downloaded from the **Online Resources** *section of this book on* **www.vibrantpublishers.com**

This page is intentionally left blank

Chapter 3

Legal and Regulatory Compliance.

A company will likely suffer legal repercussions if it does not practice policies that comply with the laws of the jurisdiction where it is located. This chapter explains the essence of legal and regulatory compliance.

It is broken down into sections that helps readers to determine the following:

- How HRM facilitates and enforces regulatory compliance in an organization

- Why a company must be compliant with the law of a jurisdiction and the general law

- Potential implications of failure to maintain legal and regulatory compliance requirements

- Some major compliance laws applicable to all organizations

Legal and regulatory compliance is now being recognized in several organizations for the sake of punishment evasion. The general idea of legal and regulatory compliance is protection. The protection applies to all faculties of an organization, including its employees and clientele. Legal compliance is the adherence to legal specifications that concern any organization.

An adequately strategized legal and regulatory compliance practice would leave a positive impact on the dealings of an organization. On the other hand, disobeying the concept will attract punishment. With the presence of a legal compliance concept, there is a high level of trust among business partners and even clients, which ensures that profit remains on a steady rise. For instance, healthcare and social networking companies are known to house a high amount of user data. Such data must not be breached, traded, or used for any commercial purpose without the user's consent. When an organization wins the trust of the client, it becomes easier to do business. Meanwhile, if a user reports a data breach, such a company will suffer legal ramifications.

Furthermore, the concept of legal and regulatory compliance couples several difficulties. An unavoidable difficulty is its constant financial requirements. To comply with legal setups means parting with cash. To keep up, an organization must employ extraordinary measures. Failure to comply with the outlined legal must-follow measures will result in punishment ranging from fines, production resources seizure, closure, and more.

Figure 3.1

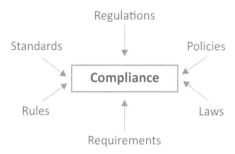

3.1 Roles of HRM in Legal and Regulatory Compliance

In the words of Koziarz, *"… compliance has created a level playing field that all organizations are expected to meet when it comes to protecting sensitive data."* This highlights the provisions accompanying the concept of legal compliance for modern organizations to follow. It has to do with data protection, employee welfare management, and the imposition of legal policies that do not breach the outstanding employment conditions. Koziarz added that *"… managing compliance takes resources, but it is nowhere near as expensive as the costs associated with a breach."* It might consume resources to be compliant with the law, but going against any order would be more costly.

Human Resource Management is a necessary department in modern organizations. The role of HRM in the aspect of legal and regulatory compliance stretches to the adherence to the regulations governing every aspect of employment. The goal is to serve as a connection between the employer-employee relationship and the law and to ensure that all company and legal policies align. Below are the roles of Human Resource Management concerning regulatory compliance.

Equilibration of Internal and External Policies

This implies that the human resource person or management team must ensure matching policies. Any policy introduced in the organization must be of a standard with that of the law and must favor both employer and employee. For this to be the case, the human resource person or department must have an understanding of the legal and regulatory laws. When the internal policies conflict with the external policies, it becomes a problem. It is worse when the organization proves difficult instead of making the internal policy correspond with that of the law. For this to be effective, Human Resource Management must identify and sort such policies.

Keep an Organization Compliant

Aspects of the organization, such as maintenance compliance like electricity, water, environmental hygiene, and gas, require specific standards. If the standard of such components within the organization do not conform with the law, the organization will suffer. The law demands that certain hazardous equipment, activities, and the atmosphere remain in good condition. Such conditions must be conducive enough for both employees and even clients to conduct transactions or to operate.

Human Resource Management helps to keep an organization in compliance with the law. Being compliant prevents unnecessary fines and limitations of any sort. On this note, the human resource team must stay conscious and fix any outlying incongruities between the organization and the legal code of conduct.

Legal Education

It is Human Resource Management's responsibility to keep an organization compliant. Since it is their responsibility, they have to participate in legal and regulatory training and education in order to stay abreast of changes. Such changes should then be transferred or shifted to the organization. If any handbooks or similar documents in the organization contain compliance policies, they must be updated or new ones made available or issued with updated compliant policies.

Protecting Employee Values

One of the primary roles of Human Resource Management is employer-employee relationship protection. Extensively, the clientele aspect of such an organization should be positively affected by the policies. Human Resource Management must ensure that employee values and rights in the company are not trampled upon, whether it is with policy implementation or workflow. The job conditions, as well as salary, must correspond with an initial agreement or working condition. It is against the law in any jurisdiction for the rights of employees to be deprived or disrespected by internally implemented policies of an organization.

Documenting Legal Rules and Regulations

Human resource persons must document legal rules and regulations. This documentation would often be beneficial at a later time for reference purposes. An 'employee handbook' (also referred to as a guide or manual) should contain these rules and policies and must be shared across the organization with every staff member. Also, after every training, updates must be entered into the handbook to keep the organization on course and compliant. Such a handbook must elaborately cite the policies of the organization and must be validated by a legal counsel of that jurisdiction.

Addressing Labor Compliance Issues

Various labor compliance circumstances can often lead to a misunderstanding in organizations. Such problems could reach a point where legal actions must be taken against the organization. It is the duty of human resource persons to reconcile the circumstances and assure the employees of effective policies and organizational compliance with the law.

3.2 Importance of Legal Compliance

Compliance simply refers to adherence to rules governing actions. Therefore, in business management, compliance is the adherence to the rules and policies governing the management system or approach of an organization in a particular jurisdiction.

It is a broad concept that connects with business management and that deals with the treatment of employees, customer data security, an organization's adherence to the laws of a particular business environment, and the general law. The idea of compliance is to ensure that an establishment – small, medium, or large, act in concordance to the law. This is to evade the punishment that accompanies the disobedience of the law. The punishment could be monetary, limitations, ban, or deprivation of any kind.

These are the underlying reasons why it is critical to comply with any legal order:

Prevention of Charges

Compliance helps to deter or eliminate unnecessary charges. The importance of legal compliance extends to unwanted charges. Here, an organization will be free from recording losses to legal functions. The charge is not just monetary; it could sometimes be a ban, limitation, suspension, withdrawal of operational right, and a refusal to recognize such an organization in the country.

Furthermore, the charges depend on the sort of incompliance. This is to say that a particular default attracts a certain charge. However, some faults carry equal punishments by the law. With compliance, all of this can be evaded while a company focuses on the growth of its business.

Establishment of Trust

Trust is one of the concepts that keep an organization thriving in society. Where the law of a particular jurisdiction pronounces an organization as 'not trustworthy,' it affects the entire structure of such an organization. The effect could range from loss of skilled workers, loss of clients, and overall disregard by the business environment. With this, productivity declines, and the aim of the organization, which is profit-making, also dies. Simple compliance can prevent an organization from losing tracks and falling into this tragedy. The human resource management team should ensure that all the dealings of the organization comply with the legal policies of the jurisdiction.

Preservation of Integrity

Any organization needs to be compliant with the legal order of jurisdiction. Reputation in a company has a huge role to play in the company's success. If the company is declared unsound, it will lose its integrity and might take longer to rebuild. A company must comply with the standards set by the law in order to be rated and recognized as healthy in the business field. In situations where there is a misunderstanding with employees, the human resource person(s) should step in and reconcile the situation. Internal policies should also be reviewed that may disagree with the law to keep and promote the integrity of the company.

Retention of a Skillful Workforce

The workforce of an organization is the brain behind its productivity. This is a component of any organization that keeps an organization at a competitive advantage. For the competitive prowess of a company to stay alive, a skilled workforce must be present. If a company does not operate in compliance with the guidelines of the law, it will be difficult to retain skilled workers, recruit or even attract able workers. It is thus advisable for a company to review its approaches and policies whenever there are signs of conflict. A company should comply by making provisions for a conducive working environment for employees, convincing employees to stay committed, and rewarding excellent employees.

3.3 Implications of Defaulting with Regulations

As an organization, defaulting regulations attract a two-way disrespect. The disrespect will become evident from both the lawmakers and the employees. This is in line with Mohammad Ali's words that you, "...*should be obedient to your superior, and your inferior will obey you.*" That is to say that disrespecting the law means losing respect from employees as well.

The law, in most cases, does not respect defaulters in that it treats everyone as equal. As long as the policies of the organization fail to comply with that of the laws of the jurisdiction, it becomes the default and is subject to punishment. A Human Resource Management team should be wary of this so that the organization does not lose track and face charges because of its conflicting policies. Here are the implications of defaulting with legal regulations, which should be avoided at all costs in any organization.

Hefty Charges

When a company defaults with regulations, the company will be charged for the act. The charges often leave significant and noticeable effects on the company, depending on its severity. A management team tasked with company policy compliance should always ensure that the different company approaches do not conflict. Where there are defaults, the company should ensure that there is a resolution before it takes court procedures. Every company should be able to identify and solve a problem at all times to avoid charges which can greatly impact the company's wallet. It is better to practice compliance policies and spend little rather than breach any standing law because the cost is usually expensive.

Limitation of Company Activities

The court has the right to punish any offender by limiting the engagements of the offender. This applies to default companies who fail to practice standards that comply with the demands of the law. A defaulting company will be ordered or expelled from several engagements that may affect its yield. Such a company may witness a slow or rapid decline in productivity, which results in a low yield.

Loss of Skilled Employees

A defaulting company risks losing skillful employees as such employees do not want to risk their individual ethics or morality at the cost of the company's failure to comply with laws. Additionally, the working atmosphere can be greatly compromised and result in a lack of production, lack of trust, or even employee burnout. One of the causes could be when a company does not standardize its policy on hygiene, electrical, gas, or water. All of these are hazardous and would force employees to sign out of the company.

Decline in Productivity

A productive organization recognizes and obeys the standing laws of a jurisdiction. This suggests that such an organization obeys the policies set by the law and practice policies that conform to the jurisdiction. One such is the proper treatment of staff by providing the necessary working tools and resources. Other aspects include recognition, encouragement, and reward for employees with high performance during a given period. Encouraging such performance means complying with employee treatment standards and will convince the employee to remain committed. Whereas, in some instances, noncompliance will result in low productivity and defaulting of the law governing the employer-employee working terms.

Fractured Reputation and Loss of Customers

Noncompliant companies often end up with the fate of losing valuable customers. "A bad name" is the result for most companies. Further, it might take a long time to effectively rebuild and correct the impression.

3.4 Maintenance of Legal and Regulatory Compliance

Maintenance is a culture of preservation. In resource management and legal compliance, it concerns the preservation of the factors deemed relevant by the law. This highly constitutes employment agreements and resources and tools required for work efficiency. An organization should have these standards in place, which must not conflict but comply with what the law demands. To go against or to be unable to attain the required standards is punishable and treated as an offense.

As Koziarz commented, it will be less expensive to manage or maintain resources in a way that complies with the jurisdiction. In the same vein, it will be costly when compensating for the law after a default or a breach. There are several compliance laws to know and preserve. If possible, request from the appropriate jurisdiction or governing agency or search online for the requirements of the jurisdiction where the organization is situated.

Meanwhile, here are some of the major compliance laws applicable to all organizations:

Electrical

The 1989 Electricity at Work Regulations charges organizations to practice a maintenance culture that curbs electrical hazards in the workplace. All electrical conditions must be excellent, and actions such as testing portable appliances must be carried out to ensure full functionality.

All of these are implemented in a bid to prevent any life hazard. Companies who do not practice this standard for electrical management, risk being punished by the law. It is a practice in most organizations to hire companies that specialize in this for a proper report.

Water

Dirty grounds and surfaces must be flushed against life-threatening infections. The standard set by the law is to treat stagnant water or do away with stagnant water in any premises. All surfaces must be kept, proper water channels must be designed, and leakages of any kind must be prevented or fixed.

There must be no wastage of water resources, and water must be available for both domestic and industrial purposes. Registered agencies must be hired to run an assessment on the facility to ascertain water health, fix broken water pipes, and ensure that it conforms or complies with the standard.

Gas

The Gas Safety Regulations 1998 presses the need to frequently check on gas systems for the safety of people. Gas leakages must be uncovered, and replacements made instantly. Commercial gas equipment must be of good condition and must always be functional and should not be left to be a housing for rodents and insects. To identify and cut down inconveniencing breakages and breakdown, checks must be done by certified engineers or a licensed engineering agency.

Hygiene

The Health and Safety Act 1974 impresses the sound hygiene of working premises. The environment must be clean and unpolluted with sources of any kind. There must be appropriate disinfectants and antibacterial products provided in bathrooms and other necessary rooms. Both customers and employees must experience a good-natured atmosphere, and there should be no littering and exposed waste ground on the premises of an organization.

Chapter Summary

◆ Legal compliance is targeted at ensuring proper treatment and security of all employees.

◆ Ensuring that a company is compliant benefits a company both within and outside the organization.

◆ Non-compliance or defaulting on legal requirements can result in substantial charges or limited company activities. Some major compliance laws applicable to all organizations include electrical, water, gas and hygiene standards.

Quiz 3

1. **Which of the following is not a critical reason to comply with legal orders?**

   a. To embrace the universalistic theory of HRM

   b. To retain a skilled workforce

   c. To preserve integrity and reputation

   d. To prevent unnecessary charges

2. **_____ HR policies should align with laws, and should serve the interest of _____, _____, and _____.**

   a. External, the employee, the customers, the board

   b. Internal, the employee, the company, the law

   c. Internal, the employee, the law, the customers

   d. External, the employee, the law, the company

3. **All of the following are compliance laws that apply to all organizations, except:**

   a. Hygiene

   b. Water

   c. Gas

   d. Temperature

4. Failure to comply with legal and regulatory compliance can result in: [select all that apply]

a. Fines

b. Resource seizures

c. Company closure

d. Customer impression of the company

e. None of the above

5. Select the statement that is True.

a. Compliance requires only medium and large organizations to adhere to laws. Smaller organizations are exempt because they have not firmly established their role as a financially sound organization.

b. Punishments for noncompliance are limited to monetary fees or fines.

c. An organization that defaults on regulations will experience a lack of respect from employees.

d. Noncompliant organizations should not be concerned with the impact on customers because the issue is internal and only involves the company and the law.

Solutions to the above questions can be downloaded from the **Online Resources** *section of this book on* **www.vibrantpublishers.com**

Chapter 4

Organizational Development In HRM

C hapter four presents the concept of Organizational Development (OD) and its correlation with Human Resource Management. OD refers to working strategies aimed at improving a company. Organizational Development is a broad concept.

This section provides readers with fundamental information that reveals the following:

- The definition and ideology of OD

- HRM goals for integrating OD in its managerial system

- OD methodological processes

- Strategic planning concepts and why it is necessary

The term 'organizational development' refers to the scientific methods and processes employed to aid in the development of an organization. It is a methodological approach towards achieving a goal, and that involves all aspects of a company. It refers to the gradual and practical development of the various faculties of an organization and looks to identify what works and what does not. The faculties may include employee performance, organization's compliance with the law, the effectiveness of the internal and external policies on an organization, and its overall productivity.

The idea of organizational development in Human Resource Management focuses on changes that could develop available human resources. It looks to replace older policies with new policies that can be effective in an organization's workforce. This often takes place in a very systemic and organized pattern as either designed by a team of human resource persons or a visionary employer of labor.

The ideology of organizational development in Human Resource Management preaches human resources development. This has a connection with the fact that human resources are a necessary aspect of the productive prowess of any organization. In short, human resources are the backbone of any organization. Human resources merit recognition from the ideology of organizational development in management due to its importance in productivity. Without productivity, which determines output, an organization would not be able to maintain its ability to perform and produce effectively. Also, unskilled or ineffective labor will discourage the growth of an establishment, and for this reason, there must be systemic standards employed by the human resource person(s) to reconcile things.

4.1 Concept of Organizational Development

The concept of organizational development (OD) is an earnest attempt to amend or better develop an organization's practical approaches and policy standard or pattern of operation. It takes place with the employment of a more sophisticated approach and relies on theories or models and a series of researches to function. The entire process is well-planned and designed before being applied to the organization for results.

Cummings and Worley (1997, p.2) posit that *"organization development is a system-wide application of behavioral science knowledge to the planned development and reinforcement of organizational strategies, structures, and processes for improving an organization's effectiveness."* This definition highlights that OD rallies around the systemically planned development to identify, solve, generate, and implement a more effective strategy to solve problems.

In the same vein, Burke (1982) asserts that *"organizational development is a planned process of change in an organization's culture through the utilization of behavioral science, technology, research, and theory."* Just like Cummings and Worley, the entire concept of organizational development relies on a system and is procedural. This means that the entire actions are carefully crafted and done in order to find the problem. Once the problem is identified, it becomes easy to solve since it has been well identified.

Consider Beckhard's view of the concept of organizational development before emphasizing the major terms. Beckhard (1969, p.9) claims that *"organizational development is an effort planned, organization-wide, and managed from the top, to increase organization effectiveness and health through planned interventions in an organization's processes, using behavioral-science knowledge."*

There are common expressions used in all of these definitions. These terms also happen to give a fuller description of the concept of organizational development. Let's identify the terms to break down the description of organizational development further. The common terms in the above definitions include:

- Science

- Plan

- System

- Process

- Development

- Change

- Effectiveness

Taking a closer look at the identified central terms, one would notice that they each have something in common. It is further proof that the concept of organizational development is purely scientific. If planned outside of scientific measures, the result might not turn out as expected.

4.2 Objectives of HRM Development

The objectives of Human Resource Management development differ from organization to organization. Several organizations each have their goal and reasons why development is important to them. Remember, the concept of Human Resource Management development thrives on the effectiveness of an idea and a scientific approach made towards it for a better result in an organization.

In most cases, the idea is interrelated with the managerial doctoring. It is a buildup and attempt to solve a problem, propose, and initiate an approach that leads to expectations. How this works is simple. First, a plan is made, and the necessary facilities of an organization are informed. Everyone is made to brace up or stay abreast of an innovative idea that will first be used in a trial and error mode. During the process, the focus switches to make a clearer definition that seems to find out whether there are flaws in the plan that an organization can do away or cope with. This is the diagnosis stage, where everything is purely experimental in the organization. During this experimental approach, ideas are retrieved, and these ideas are such that they could be very effective in the organization.

Since the goal of a developmental strategy is to identify and use what works, the extracted ideas will then be tested in some faculties with expectancy that it works. Often, a well-strategized and properly developed developmental structure works.

Competitive Human Resource Management can figure this out and use it in an organization. Moreover, different strategies work for different organizations, and this is due to the overall operational, in-place policy, theoretical approach of a company. This would not be an impossible target for any talented Human

Resource Management team.

This said, after the effectiveness of human resources development in an establishment, there are fundamental expectations. Principally, these are the objectives of management development. Here are the targets and objectives of Human Resource Management development in an establishment.

Increasing Profits

Profit maximization remains an undeniable concept in any development campaign. It concerns, as earlier identified, approaches that encourage more profit. Several strategies, like staff training, policy review, legal and regulatory compliance, as well as staff encouragement, are taken into consideration. These help a company to maximize profit and remain in business.

Setting an Organization on a Competitive Advantage

Dale S. Beach perceives organization development as *"a complex educational strategy designed to increase organizational effectiveness and wealth through planned intervention by a consultant using theory and techniques of applied behavioral service."* As seen here, the foremost objective of organization development is effectiveness and wealth. The idea of wealth awakens the sense that a company adopts this strategy to increase profit, which is the basis of any establishment, by attempting to initiate measures that boost its chances over those of other competitors.

Employee Growth

Since the aim of organization development is the betterment of an organization, strategies like staff development also emerge. When a company shifts recognition to staff's growth, it grows the business too. The productive aspect of any establishment relies on employees and not just employees but resourceful employees. For there to be resourceful employees, there must be employee training, a conducive working environment, recognition and reward, and respect of employee and initial working conditions.

Enhanced Communication

With the effectiveness of the concept of organization development, there will be an enhanced communication and communication channels. There will as well be a healthy employer-employee relationship encouraged through proper communication. Undoubtedly, without effective communication, a company will remain stiff and unyielding. The leaders at the top and middle will find it incredibly difficult to communicate with the workforce and identify problems that require a solution.

4.3 Processes of Organizational Development

The processes of organizational development refer to the simple step by step approach structured by an organization to achieve a desirable goal. These processes are aimed at attaining a height that exceeds the initial benchmark of an organization. They are scientifically done in an organized manner and require attention to all aspects of the establishment in order to evade confusing goals with another. The entire possible result lies in the operational force of the management. Moreover, whatever plan is designed must align because a misalignment could break the entire buildup, thereby resulting in an unexpected and unwanted result. The processes could well differ depending on the objectives or focused goal of a company.

However, these general methodological processes are usually implemented for better results:

Sorting Problems

The first process in organizational management is problem diagnosis or sorting. It involves uncovering the setbacks, avoidance, and establishing policies. Problem identification must be carried out with attentiveness because of its sensitivity. Where possible, both human and nonhuman tools must be used to figure out an exact cause. It is recommendable to closely study four categories, including the employer, management, workforce, and company policies. These are the four categories that encompass problems likely to disentangle the process or the company.

Examination of the Diagnosed Problem(s)

This should immediately follow after sorting or diagnosing problems. There should be close scientific research on the outlying problem. In this phase, studies warn that it is abysmal to be partial with the situation. This means that no problematic faculty of the company must be overlooked, whether it is the employer, the management, employees, or the nonhuman resources. The moment the source of a problem is favored, it becomes a 'problem suspended.' On this note, such a problem must be revisited and corrected, or the result will be awful.

Collection of Relevant Data

Each of the identified problems has a source. The sources must be the focal point from this instant. That is, any department guilty of a problem must be put under close supervision for relevant data to be retrieved. This could be done in the form of retrieving daily or weekly activities report from such a department. Do note that only relevant data, as suggested, must be retrieved. Other than this, the systematic approach will be lost, and the entire process will become complicated.

Scrutinizing and Planning

After retrieving relevant activity or policy data, set up and task a team with the scrutiny of such data. Inform the team on what to do and ensure that the individual progress is monitored once in a while. The importance of allotting this task to a managerial team is because running the scrutiny along might turn out inaccurate. Next, retrieve a report from the team and collate it as a team. Effect a plan that agrees with the problem.

Implementation of Plan

After gathering the necessary information and coming up with a suitable plan, make a draft for clarity. Forward the plan to each of the affected departments and make sure that the newly effected plan is followed. From time to time, review and examine the progress.

Retrieval of Implemented Plan Data

After a given time, retrieve data of the implemented plan.

Look out for improvements and figure out why it changed. Make amendments or revisions to the new policy, deepening on the target. Monitor the progress until the end of the business period, where the appraisal will be done.

Analyze Results

At the end of a business period, confirm the result, and identify positives. Write out all positives alongside the effective strategy accompanying it. Analyze the result and move it on to the next business season. For plan actions that resulted in less favorable outcomes, revisit the strategies to determine if there should be amendments or discontinuation of certain processes.

4.3.1 Strategic Planning

An organization cannot sustain growth and success without a working strategy. Strategy defines or describes the method in which a series of actions are being utilized with the sole aim of achieving a goal. When a company strategizes, there is a height that such a company intends to reach. As such, the concept of strategic planning evolves.

Defining Strategic Planning

This term originates from strategy, and it refers to a simple plan of action. It is an arrangement of ideas, policies, and finally, a decisive measure taken towards achieving a feat in an organization. The primary aim of strategic planning is to ensure the utility of only what works. If a strategy, which is often targeted at the improved output, fails, it suggests that planning is absent or there is improper managerial planning. However, when the strategy works, it entails that the management has gone deeper into finding what works, and this is done procedurally.

In the course of strategic planning, we can refer to the strategizing team as strategists. Their job is straightforward, and the difficulty depends on the skills of the individuals involved.

Strategists are conventionally expected to be systematic with their dealings. Several approaches must be put in place to plan out a strategy for an establishment. This is the reason because the concept of strategic planning thrives on evolution from what is unyielding towards what will yield. With the following said, let's identify the necessary procedures towards enacting or planning a working strategy for the increased productivity of any organization.

Processes of Strategic Planning

Below are the traditional processes towards planning a strategy:

Formulation

This stage merely involves identifying an action before plans are made. Once identified, what follows is another simple arrangement of ideas of what is to be employed as a strategy. For example, if a company wishes to set up internal policies, they have to come up with ideas that will make such policies comply with the legal standard of a jurisdiction.

Execution

This stage involves applying the generated plan into the process. The process here refers to what is needed for the strategy to be used.

Evaluation

During this stage, management should follow up on the implemented plans to ascertain whether it is working or not.

Why Strategic Planning is Necessary

Some organizations fail to realize the need for strategic planning. As a result, such companies often end up on the wrong end of expectations. For example, a company that seeks to perform well but is unable to map out a strategy to enhance such a motive would fail. It should be a norm in any big establishment to own a specialized department focused on strategic planning to remain or last in the game.

Here are the reasons why strategic planning is necessary:

- Effectiveness of policies in an organization

- Enhanced output

- Enactment of intelligible policies

- Increased productivity

- Ability to comply with the legal standard of a jurisdiction

- A conforming and organized way of management

- In some cases, the recruitment of highly skilled individuals

4.3.2 Recruitment

Human Resource Management must be knowledgeable about recruitment. Recruitment involves the intake of human resources for production to take place. However, the concept of recruitment requires a strategic plan of action. That is, it has to be scientific;

otherwise, it will impact the organization negatively. For instance, a company that recruits but that recruits unskilled individuals will find productivity and output on a steady decline. Going by this, it suffices to maintain that the contribution of proper recruitment must not go unrecognized in any environment. How can this proper requirement be achieved? As mentioned earlier, it should follow a scientific process to arrive with the right hands, which means more significant outputs.

DeCenzo and Robbins have their say on recruitment. According to these scholars, *"Recruitment is the process of discovering the potential for actual or anticipated organizational vacancies."* However, their definition fails to highlight that the discovery must be skilled since an unskilled discovery will be useless to the growth of an organization unless there is an otherwise investment in training and developing the talent.

With an emphasis on skills, Yoder's definition provides what we need. For Yoder, *"Recruitment is a process to discover the sources of manpower to meet the requirements of the staffing schedule and to employ effective measures for attracting that manpower in adequate numbers to facilitate effective selection of an efficient working force."* Taking a closer look at Yoder's opinion, recruitment must basically be a selection of the best 'skilled' individuals. In management, failure to have a highly skilled and committed workforce would mean 'zero' and 'decline.'

Process of Recruitment

Since recruitment is a necessary force in an organization, it must be strategic and procedural.

Identify the Needed Position

The first thing is to identify the vacant position in the organization. Note, identifying a position does not necessarily mean it must be empty. This implies that recruitments could be done into areas that require human resource support. That is, another employee is needed to boost the productive prowess of a particular position.

Outline Its Demands

What does such a position demand? How skillful enough must the potential employee be? These and many more are the questions to answer in order to be able to outline the demands of the required position properly. Moreover, it is wise to ensure that a particular position does not inhabit substances that make it a complicated condition. For this to be unveiled, a human resource person must visit both internal and external policies to make sure they do not conflict and are legally compliant.

Generate a Clear Description of the Job

The description must be clear enough for potential employees to understand what they are signing up to do. Consult the former employees of such a position for further information for a better description of the offer.

Source and Screen

The final thing to do is to source and screen individuals. Be careful not to screen in the wrong candidate. Here are tips that might be helpful while screening applicants for the position:

- Applicant qualifications must be in line what the description

- Applicant must be fluent with the atmosphere

- Whether experienced or not, an applicant must be able to state what he or she would likely do in difficult and demanding circumstances of the job.

If necessary, break the screening into stages. This will further help to eliminate the wrong hands and minds. There are a series of interview methods available. While the traditional interview method works for some organizations, the behavioral interview method works better for others. It will depend on the sort of company in place to decide which interview approach to employ.

Review the Candidate Performance

After making selections, consider checking in on and reviewing the progress of the newly employed staff on a regular or consistent basis. Where necessary, train such staff to become better in the field. It is necessary to introduce new staff to the already existing staff. This should help provide rooms for quicker learning and a more community structured environment. Moreover, staff-staff learning works best as there is an absence of intimidation. Most companies practice this to aid their staff to learn and adapt fast for an increased yield.

4.3.3 Enforcing Compliance

Compliance is an act of carrying out activities, enacting policies, and giving out treatments that agree with the outlined standard. Concerning organizations, to comply means to have policies that do not conflict with the laws of the jurisdiction. Several enforcement agencies are fixedly looking for organizations that will disregard the principles of the law. Such organizations are said to operate in a noncompliant manner, which is punishable.

Compliance agencies are primarily tasked with maintaining compliance across a jurisdiction. The agency receives complaints about organizations, set out to investigate and review such complaints. Where an organization is found guilty, maybe for the use of things like water and gas in a way that does not conform with the regulatory rules, such an organization will be punished. Apart from material noncompliance, an establishment could be noncompliant concerning human resources. For example, failure to provide a standard working environment or disregard for initial working conditions will deem an organization to have violated the law.

From a managerial perspective, compliance should remain a focal point, no matter what happens. The activities, policies, and even employee treatment must comply with the standard norm. Any government policy disrespected for any cause will only draw unnecessary negative effects on the company. Based on how the law is structured, such might even lead to a decline in a company's productive prowess.

A human resource team must ensure that the company policies do not conflict with the law. Regular consultations must be made to any document encompassing the legal standards to keep the company on course. Also, abiding by the law of jurisdiction may come with expenses. Nevertheless, violating the law is very costly and can put a company out a competitive advantage for a long while.

4.4 Benefits of Organizational Development

The development of a company depends excessively on the management. Sometimes, when a company fails to deliver massively, the blame is shifted to the managerial teams. In truth, the managerial element is responsible for organizational development such that they are liberated with authority to sort and implement what works.

The aim is to move a company or an establishment from an area of low performance to an area of high performance. This involves the employer, employee, management, and even production resources.

For an organization to grow, such an organization must have a clearly illustrated setting that encourages development beginning from the emotional aspect of the stakeholders. Organizational development is vital in many ways.

Below are four basic advantages of organizational benefits:

Employee Growth

A primary goal of companies is to maximize profits. Even with the right resources, the absence of human resources cannot actualize this vision. Therefore, an employee must be there to actualize the vision since he or she is the mind of the productiveness of the organization. On this note, organizational development tends to focus on the growth of the employee in order to establish a proper workforce for profiting.

Improved Employer-Employee Relationship

The concept equally helps to strengthen the relationship between workers and their employers. It creates a link for effective communication to take place, thereby boosting productivity, morale, commitment, and work environment.

Steady and Rising Output

Apart from profit-making, companies try to gain a competitive advantage over others. This is necessary because the more authority an organization builds, the more prominent and relevant it becomes in society. Organizational development plays a role by confronting and expelling the challenges that could hinder the rapid progress of an organization.

Regulatory/Legal Compliance

Law agencies detest companies that violate standards. Companies equally detest being caught in the act knowing the consequences accompanying such. Organizational development then attempts to review and ensure that both organizational and legal policies do not conflict.

Chapter Summary

◆ Organizational Development is a strategic process that refers to the gradual and practical development of the various faculties of an organization and looks to identify what works and what does not.

◆ Strategic planning, recruitment, and compliance enforcement are three pivotal parts of organizational development.

◆ Strategic planning involves three traditional stages which include formulation, execution and evaluation.

◆ The various processes that result in a proper recruitment practice should involve the identification of a vacant position, outlining the requirements of the position, generating a description of job, sourcing and screening and finally reviewing the performance of the recruit.

◆ Enhanced communication, employee growth, competitive advantage, and increased profits are all objectives of HRM development.

Quiz 4

1. **Which series of words most accurately complete the definition of Organizational Development? "Organization development is a _____ process to help a(n) _____ reach goals."**

   a. strategic, organization

   b. scientific, employee

   c. methodical, organization

   d. conceptual, employee

2. **What is the appropriate order of the general procedural processes that are implemented for better results when considering organizational development?**

   a. Collect data, sort problems, examine diagnosed problems, scrutinize and plan, implement plans, retrieve plan data, & analyze results

   b. Collect data, retrieve plan data, sort problems, examine diagnosed problems, scrutinize and plan, implement plans, & analyze results

   c. Sort problems, examine diagnosed problems, collect data, scrutinize and plan, implement plans, retrieve plan data, & analyze results

   d. Sort problems, examine diagnosed problems, collect data, retrieve plan data, scrutinize and plan, implement plans, & analyze results

3. **All of the following are reasons strategic planning is necessary, except:**

   a. Enhanced output

   b. Increased productivity

   c. Policy effectiveness

   d. To avoid employee challenges

4. **Which of the following are objectives of HRM development? [select all that apply]**

   a. Employee growth

   b. Setting a company on a competitive advantage

   c. Terminating poor performers

   d. Increasing Profits

   e. All of the above

5. Enhancing the relationship between _____ and
   _____ creates a link for better communication. This
   enhancement leads to increased productivity, _____,
   _____, and work environment

   a. employee, employee, sacrifice, tenure

   b. employer, employee, morale, commitment

   c. employer, stakeholder, turnover, loyalty

   d. employer, employee, morale, retention

Solutions to the above questions can be downloaded from
the **Online Resources** *section of this book on*
www.vibrantpublishers.com

Chapter 5

Conflict Management

Conflict is an unavoidable happening in any organization and may be initiated by an individual or group. Chapter five focuses on highlighting conflict and the various approaches that could dissolve it.

This chapter provides readers with competency to explain the following:

- Definition and examples of conflict

- Characteristics of conflict

- The effects of conflict and the need to avoid it

- Different classifications of conflict

- Conflict resolution approaches and strategies

- Factors engendering conflict within an organization

An organization relies on the peaceful coexistence of human resources, management, and the employer to do well. When there is a conflict between these groups, it forces the effect of underperformance, which leads to a low yield. A conflict could also be initiated by or involve other stakeholders such as customers, clients, boards, or volunteers. Therefore, a conflict must be avoided like a plague in any business setting or organization for any planned target to be possible.

Conflict is anything that attracts unrest in an organized system. It is often a reaction to unfavorable policies. In a managerial sense, conflict is simply a deliberate agitating measure taken towards a plan of action or action in a company. It is often notable among human resources but prevalent in other faculties of an organization as well.

Definition and Difficulties of Conflict Management

Conflict management is a reactive measure taken to weigh down the effects of conflict on a company's general performance. The concept identifies the source of a problem, proffer, and implements a solution. Could conflict have a connection with compliance? Many human resource persons have at a time, wondered about the connection between conflict and regulatory compliance. The simple response is that as long as the laws of jurisdiction are against conflict, it applies to managerial, employee, and employer conflicts in organizations.

Moreover, conflict management is a scientific-based concept. The reason is that it requires measures and steps to be taken in managing the causes of underperformance, imbalance relationship, and low yield in an organization. Without a quick response to conflict or an attempt towards conflict management, many difficulties will arise. Some of the difficulties include the following.

Weak Communication

Conflict does not encourage communication. Thus, it promotes a poor relationship between management, employers, and employees. Conflict in an organization is synonymous with a society that is not interactive. This is the case because it often leads to a misunderstanding that might result in a fight. The absence of communication will not just affect the relationship of the organization but that of the customers too. In cases where such conflict is noticeable, customers might withdraw their patronage.

Underperformance

A lively organization features a committed workforce. However, when the workforce encounters conflict, it takes away the spark and willingness to be committed and dedicated to a task. Naturally, it attracts a dull environment that does not encourage productivity. A conflict-ridden organization does not encourage employee development as there is no functional relationship to enhance such.

Low Productivity

It is a norm in any organization for conflict to encourage low productiveness. It will be surprising for a conflict-ridden organization to perform well in any faculty. In a business environment, there is a provision of the chart indicating company growth; such a company would often find itself sloping downwards and remaining at a low level. This equally signifies that such an organization is inactive in the in-place competition. Subsequently, they are out of the environmental competition for better control of the business environment.

5.1 Features of Conflict

Although conflict is inevitable, organizations inflicted by conflict can always get through with proper understanding and reconciliation from conflicting parties. It is ideal to reconcile conflicts because they can ruin any existing relationship in a company in a blink of an eye.

Moreover, conflict in an organization might sometimes be a movement towards a new standard. This means that conflict has the potential to build after destroying. An organization that recently reconciled differences among themselves will notice that there will be some sort of tolerance that initially lacked before and during the conflict. Unlike several other concepts, a conflict has things that define it.

Inevitability

Any organization should be well prepared, as an absolute is that within an operating business construct, conflict is inevitable. No matter how organized an organization is, the challenge of conflict will always set in. It could be management-employer conflict, employer-employee conflict, employee-employee, or management-employee conflict. These are collectively called inter-organizational conflicts. There is also an intra-organizational conflict that involves employees. However, what defines organizational management is its ability to reconcile differences.

Avoidable

This implies that with the right measures, conflict can be put out or minimized within and outside of the organization. Most companies set up teams other than resource management teams to identify and expel conflicts from the organization regularly. In cases where the managerial department is not proactive towards conflict, a conflict will arise. When it does, it will require an enormous strategy and resources to reconcile. It is better to design a proactive strategy that keeps checking on a conflict from eventually taking place.

Reconciliation

The idea is that conflict is not a concept that completely locks down a company but a necessary happening that can be solved whenever it arises. Conflict occurs as a process and can be solved procedurally. All it takes is a well-planned strategy that convinces the involved parties of the need to reconcile an outstanding misunderstanding. Whether it is internal or external, a sufficing resolution is not far-fetched. Also, it is easier to fix an internal conflict than external conflict. The reason is that externally conflicting parties likely have contradictory policies that will more than often disagree.

Noticeable

Companies with problems cannot conceal their problems. This brings on a soured competition, and the conflict would always be noticeable in the way both companies deal with each other's affairs. If it is in an environment with multiple establishments of the same niche, the other companies will seize the opportunity to become competitively better.

Spreads Rapidly

Conflict spreads rapidly. It is like a communicable disease, and several companies or individuals can become involved. In an organization, for instance, when conflict arises, it moves from table to table. While moving, other personalities in the company will take sides. The supporters for each individual will tend to dislike the individuals supporting the other. This also happens on an organizational level where companies pick sides and rebuke the other company. This will arise in opposition and could affect the entire business health of a business environment. Such should be resolved on time to avoid low productivity.

5.2 Classification of Conflict

Occasionally, conflicts arise in workplaces. The scope behind conflict usually is on who is right and who is wrong. Both parties often tend to think they are right while ignoring the fact that both could be wrong. David L. Austin (1976) opines that *"It can be defined as a disagreement between two or more individuals or groups, with each individual or group trying to gain acceptance of its view or objectives over others."*

Drawing from Austin's opinion, it is evident that organizational conflicts are founded on personal objectives. Most times, neither party wants to listen to the other but, instead, feel they are right. This sort of conflict arises on various basis. It could be based on strategy, result, involvement, or scope. Whichever way, the focal point remains that conflict occurs because the involved or conflicting parties in an organization have refused to listen to each other's views and objectives and to accept them in one form or another. As long as either party values only its objectives, the conflict will persist.

Traditionally, the scope conflict is broad and so are its types. Some of the types of conflict include relationship conflict, value conflict, task conflict, intra-organizational conflict, inter-organizational conflict, interpersonal conflict, intrapersonal conflict.

Relationship Conflict

This has to do with the soured relationships between either employers and employees, employers and management, management-employee, or even employee and employees. The basis of conflicts such as this arises when the means of communication goes sour. It becomes tough to handle happiness, and as such, the organization loses. To fix a conflict such as this, human resource management must identify and reconcile the conflicting parties. Such would be possible through effective communication strategies.

Value Conflict

The differences in values are causative reasons why conflict takes place. This is most notable among the management staff since they are responsible for the planning of policies in the organization. A management team might consist of various individuals with varying beliefs. In most instances, such individuals tend to require that their suggestions be recognized over those of others. Sometimes, it could be as a result of personal interest.

Task Conflict

This is a type of conflict that arises when there is a difficulty or vast difference in the task apportioned. It is often a conflict of employer-employee, employer-management, or management-employee. For example, when the staff has a shared duty, it might initially appear as a simple task. Eventually, it becomes tougher and, in most cases, beyond the working conditions. The employee may experience difficulty and attempt to express it to management. Whereas management believes they have already mapped out or devised the perfect tasks to support the organization, an employee may vehemently disagree.

Interpersonal and Intrapersonal Conflicts

Interpersonal conflict occurs between two persons in an organization. It is usually among staff with varying belief systems. Sometimes, it has to do with external affairs that do not concern the organization. Also, it is as a result of differences in how both individuals view certain things. For example, if an employee is apportioned a task, another employee might arrive with a different idea thinking the initial idea is substandard or would be ineffective. On the other hand, intrapersonal conflict refers to the difficulties within one's mind in an organization. Such difficulties could be conflicting thoughts towards a standing policy. It often ends in weak participation of such employees in the organization.

Intergroup and Intragroup Conflicts

Unlike interpersonal and intrapersonal conflicts, intergroup and intragroup conflict involve a team or a group in an organization. Intergroup conflict is common in organizations featuring teams tasked with a different responsibility that should boost the organization's business performance. For example, a conflict might arise with the welfare department and social duties department in an organization. The social group department might then pick up issues with the welfare department due to probably the issuance of an amount that does not meet requirements. The different group might be thinking their initial demand is outrageous while the demanding team thinks they are trying to cheat. Intragroup conflict is different. This conflict occurs in a team of workers tasked with a goal. The only difference between intergroup and intragroup conflict is that intergroup occurs between two or more different groups, while intragroup occurs within the same team or group.

Moreover, knowing what conflict an organization suffers helps to design a strategy that can be a fix. Conflict, however, can be classified based on result, involvement, scope, strategy, and a few more.

5.2.1 Conflict Based on Result

When conflict occurs based on the result, it could be very unappealing to the required goals. It is a destructive event that encourages confusion in a single team or among multiple teams or groups in an organization. Most organizations are designed to maximize profits. This is a well-known scope in the establishment of various enterprises. Furthermore, for a company to maximize profits, there must be planned strategic approaches. In this case, vast resource managerial manpower is required to put everything on a course to success. For example, the Human Resource Management of an organization would be tasked with the responsibility of looking after or managing the human workforce aspect of an organization to achieve a result. For success, there must be no conflict, because conflict will kill the vision towards a result.

When conflict sets into an organization, it sparks destruction. It takes away the needed recognition and introduces a tainted atmosphere. Necessary activities might be suspended or called off because conflict based on the result makes it evident that a planned goal cannot be attained in such a condition. How does this happen? An individual, a team, or an organization will be emotionally polarized. Furthermore, such an individual, team, or organization's morale would be undermined. There could be an outbreak of fights, quarrels, verbal assaults, manipulation, and conniving behavior. Imagine having clients gathered while there is an interpersonal fight among some of the staff.

Conflict on the basis of result affects a greater part of an organization. The main point, however, is that it does not matter what aspect the conflict grows from. The scope remains that it destroys every plan and puts an individual, group, and organization at a losing end.

Reassuringly, conflicts that affect results can be swept off with simple strategic plans. Here is what should be done to curb conflicts on this basis.

Identify the Source

No conflict exists without a source. The source would most certainly be known by the individuals in charge of the expected goals. Set up an investigative team of about two to three persons depending on the size of the organization. The process toward discovery should not exceed three days before the real or root cause is uncovered.

Review

At this point, the uncovered cause must be reviewed. Without reviewing such a cause, it will be challenging to know how to eradicate the happening permanently. In cases where involved individuals or groups were issued specific responsibilities to complete, the focus should be on why one of the individuals or groups despises the other. In fact, in most recorded cases, the fault is always as a result of allocating the wrong workforce to the wrong individual or team.

Implement

After a review, make amends and restart the program. A conflict does not mean an absolute end to any plan of action. It is only usually a short problematic break. For a while, monitor the newly enacted policies governing the initially conflicting cause. Check how the new program goes and ensure that nothing conflicts again with the needed result.

5.2.2 Conflict based on Involvement

On the basis of involvement, conflict takes an individual, group, or organizational aspect. No matter which of these is involved, the conflict will still leave its impact on the system. Let us break down the aspects of conflict based on involvement below.

Based on involvement in the individual aspects, there are two types, as mentioned earlier. They include:

- Interpersonal
- Intrapersonal

There is a similarity between these two aspects of individual conflict on the basis of involvement. People often confuse interpersonal conflict with intrapersonal conflict in an organization. The similarity between these two types of conflict is that both have to do with individual workers. However, the difference is that interpersonal conflict concerns, multiple individuals, while intrapersonal involves just one individual with thoughts that conflict either with a policy or plan towards a goal. Conflicts such as these are always hard on the organization because human resources are the productive minds of any organization. In order to reconcile this conflict, the affected individual or individuals should be invited for a brief review conversation. This can be done by the managerial department or even the employer, if necessary. But then, it is recommended to forward such to the human resource center for a better review and permanent resolution.

Based on involvement on group aspect, the categories include:

- Intergroup

- Intragroup

If individual conflicts hit an organization hard, group conflicts hit harder. This is not a scope but a deduction from a clear sense of judgment. Intergroup conflict is an opposition existing between multiple groups or teams in an organization. It differs from an intragroup conflict in that an intragroup conflict occurs among the members within a particular group or team in an organization. Studies suggest that intergroup conflict has a higher impact than an intragroup conflict. This statement is dependable in the sense that intergroup may likely involve a higher number of individuals than intragroup. Being that human resource is the brain behind the productiveness of every organization, an increased workforce would mean a more negative impact. The often-working strategic plan is the shuffling of such a team or group. This should come in after sorting the source of the conflict.

The third conflict that falls on the basis of involvement is organizational conflict. There are two organizational conflicts which include:

- Interorganizational

- Intraorganizational

While an interorganizational conflict involves opposition between different organizations, intraorganizational conflict is a conflict within a particular organization. Neither of these two types of conflicts has little impact on an organization. This class of conflict can well lead to the end of an organization's existence. The reason is that every faculty of the conflict is usually involved. It can be employer-employee conflict, employer-management conflict, as well as management-employee conflict. The worst is when the conflict is an inter-organizational type of conflict. The clash of two organizations will not only affect an organization or organizations, but it will also give other establishments in the same field a tremendous competitive advantage.

5.2.3 Conflict Based on Scope

Conflict on this basis may occasionally arise on cases as minor as inconveniencing meeting time decisions, a decision on who represents the organization, task allocation, and more. The list of the sort of events housing conflict based on scope is endless.

An article on 'Your Article Library' suggests that conflict could be substantive as well as effective. When conflict is substantive, it directly concerns the duties developed or that are part of an organization's policies. On this basis, whatever an employee, manager, and any other resource person does in an organization must comply with the principles of such an organization. Substantial conflict is often caused by the disaccording objectives or views of a workforce or management with the in-place objectives. This is to say that substantive conflict does not involve the opposition between an individual or a group of individuals. It, in fact, has little or nothing to do with employee or management emotions.

On the contrary, affective conflict involves individuals' relationships. This could be an emotional or concrete (physical) relationship. It equally involves a group of workforces in an organization and an organization as a whole. It thus suffices to say that an effective conflict extends from personal relationship to group relationship on to the organization level.

Between substantive and affective conflicts based on scope, substantive is the most endurable. Substantive conflict is all about organizational productivity, and it embodies an achievable goal. Whereas effective conflict is unendurable, costly, and can prevent an establishment from reaching a desired goal.

5.2.4 Conflict Based on Strategy

On the basis of strategy, conflict ensues on plans towards achieving a goal. Strategized conflict mostly comprises organizations. In rare cases, however, it involves individuals and groups of a particular organization. It can only be said to involve a party or parties of the same organization when such party or parties are tasked with objectives that must be sorted either on a competitive basis or cooperative basis. In essence, conflict based on strategy could arise either as a competition or a joint force towards achieving a goal.

Conceptually, conflict is said to be competitive when varying organizations or individuals tasked with the same objectives (the goal of such objectives would be on who gets there first or who records the better success) battle it out to see who leads at the end of the day. In a competitive conflict, what matters is a 'win.' Every involved party (organizational or individual), therefore, employs a strategy - rational or irrational, to gain an advantage over the other competitor. In the process, either party develops some sort of unconscious dislike for the other. By 'unconscious,' it means that either of the parties may not realize the hatred towards the other organization or group.

Conflict on a cooperative basis can also be referred to as collaborative conflict. It is a conflict taking place among establishments of the same objectives, same goal, and equal target. These organizations may operate as a merger and would suffer losses together as well as gain together. Despite being on the same course and having a similar pursuit, there is bound to the opposition in the long run.

Conclusively, neither a competitive nor a cooperative conflict help in the growth of organizations. Both leave negative impacts but promote competitiveness, which may either be healthy or unhealthy. However, a cooperative conflict is most recognized and practiced by several organizations in order to declare a desirable competitive ground and freedom.

5.3 Approaches to Conflict Management

After the transition from pre-industrialization to industrialization, organizational management faced yet another difficulty, which was conflict. However, several attempts have been made by managerial professionals to curb the problem. Initially planned strategies showed no positives until the discovery of the five-approach resolution techniques to conflict spearheaded in the 1970s. The reputable and intellectual names involved in the breakthrough to conflict management are Kenneth Thomas alongside Ralph Kilmann. The approach is designed with competition, accommodation, avoidance, collaboration, and compromise as cornerstones.

Conflict is suffered by several organizations today. This is as a result of its inevitable but costly avoidable nature. As a scope, it thrives on organizational destruction rather than organizational development. It affects multiple productive factors of any organization, including human resource development.

To prevent conflict from becoming the order in an organization, *here are the universally accepted approaches to adopt.*

Competing

This approach is such that triggers 'unconscious hatred' among competitors or parties. The scope is that best is the victor, and as such, every party wants to be the victor. This is not genuinely possible in the sense that in any event throttled by competitiveness, only the best wins. This approach requires enough resources and intelligence on the side of any competitor with the intent to win. Involved parties often employ strategies as rational and as irrational as possible in a bid to stay above. As such, the competition becomes burdensome to the extent that competitors have to lose to stay up. It mimics the positivity in sports like encouraging for quick thinking, faster implementations, better productivity, and ever-ready actions, among others.

Accommodating

This approach opposes competing in the sense that it functions as a subordinating merger. The idea is that, as a competitor or involved party in the conflict, one would dissolve by agreeing to circumvent the target for the opposition. It is not the most promising approach to conflict management; however, it encourages unity. But then, it might completely wipe off participation in the program. Studies have found that it is not the most actively practiced approach as it completely or partly puts one of the involved parties aside.

Avoiding

The concept here is simple. It is almost synonymous with the competing approach. However, the difference is that this approach surrenders to the other party. This may either be willingly or as a result of excessive pressure that the withdrawing party cannot resist. It is not very healthy as it discourages competitiveness and would often result in extreme domination by one party. In cases where a conflict involves two teams or groups in an organization, it might lead to the exemption of the other party. In an organizational basis, the competitive prowess and presence of a company may become desolate.

Collaborating

This implies the working together of conflicting individuals, groups, or organizations towards achieving a goal. This approach sparks some kind of unilateral operations whereby every conflicting party is subject to one another. The win of party X is a win of party Y, and the loss of party Y is a loss of party X. In essence, it is the pulling together of resources, in some cases, and following an informed course that is favorable to everyone. Moreover, for any resolution, the strategized resolving measures must be in line with the policies, beliefs, and interests of conflicting parties. Finally, it ensures a resolution that favors both parties.

Compromising

This is more like a medial alternative for avoiding and competing approaches. It draws some aspects from the mentioned approaches, and both conflicting parties contribute to the in-place plans towards resolving the conflict at hand.

Figure 5.1

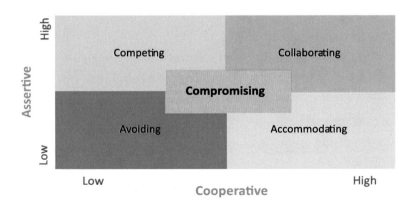

5.4 Causative Factors of Conflict

Conflict is avoidable and solvable but still inevitable. Some organizations believe that they are too perfect to experience conflict. However, this is fallacious in several angles. Conflict is not something planned for; it takes everyone off guard. It is likely to occur in organizations where there is too little or no attention paid to things that could cause problems. For example, the least substantive conflict like company policy could trigger a fallout within an individual, and this is referred to as intraindividual conflict. It leaves an employee emotionally uncomfortable, which affects the workflow of the organization. There are several other causative factors of conflict of which every management department should be aware. Knowing these factors would help to manage the organization in a way that pushes it away from being confronted by conflict. Some of the causes mentioned are in line with Bell and Hart's assertions on the causes of conflict.

Contradictory Objectives

This is the most common cause of conflict in any organization. It is this causative factor that makes it possible to assert that conflict in the workplace is inevitable. When individual objectives clash, it gives rise to a conflict in various dimensions. This is most common among organizational departments of equal category. For instance, if a group in an organization is tasked with a duty of ensuring legal compliance, members may each have ideas that disagree. As such, each of the group members will frown at the ideas of one another. At this point, such responsibility is halted because the beneficial head-start, which is a collective decision among the members, is missing.

Absence of Recognition and Reward

Money encourages people to work, but as Dale Carnegie opines, when an employee is duly recognized, he or she becomes very committed. The sort of conflict that arises in instances such as this is intraindividual conflict. It destabilizes an employee and boosts his mental laziness. This is simply because the employee's initial worthy performance was not recognized. Such an employee feels rejected and resorts to low productivity. The conflict occurs within the individual and causes such an individual to be sad or demotivated. No organization would want to house this sort of conflict because productivity from that angle will dwindle. If this is the case with half of a company's employees, it suffices to say that such an organization is underperforming.

Assigning Wrong Duty

Assigning a role to the wrong employee is yet another causative factor of conflict. It permeates fear, inconsistency (if such an employee is performing well at all), and makes an employee feel unable.

Absurd Role Description

When there is no clarity in a role description, it is difficult for either an individual, a group, or an organization as a whole to perform without leading to a conflict.

Poor Employee Development

Poor employee development conflicts in terms of work performance. An employee who is not put through a developmental process or training would either not adapt in time or fall out. Intraindividual conflict is a serious conflict category suffered by several organizations and must be evaded.

Other causative factors of conflict include:

- Incompliance with working terms

- Discrimination (e.g., gender, race, religion, education, language, role or position)

- Biased employee protection

To sort either of these cases, a proper strategic plan must be developed on the basis of trial and error. Fixing errors make it quite easy for any organization to move on swiftly with the activities that lead to high yield.

5.5 Conflict Resolution Practices

When a conflict is allowed accommodation in an organization, it results in a complete breakdown. For such reason, strategic plans to resolve these conflicts must be in place. An employer in an organization should consider defining or following the tested strategies outlined below. Moreover, it is recommendable to assign this as a responsibility to the management department for more brilliant strategy implementation.

Erect a Team to Source for Cause

If the involved parties - individual or organization, are within the company, set up a team to source for the cause of the conflict. This team could otherwise be called 'strategist,' and their near simple task is to find the cause. The difficulty in sorting a cause could be elaborate or simple, depending on the conflicting factors and conflicting parties involved. The team should set into the midst of the conflict and make inquiries. It is through these inquiries that the strategists would get access to the minds of the conflicting bodies. Before this, such a team must be well-informed of the duty or responsibility leading to the conflict. For example, if it is an opposition between two groups in an organization, their tasks must be reviewed to better understand the complaints each party will give. In cases of intraindividual conflict, a similar approach must be followed.

Invite the Conflicting Parties

This should follow immediately after the discovery of the conflict cause. Questioning parties in their task places are not enough. This time around, be it a group of individuals or an individual, they must be tabled, in most cases, with a disciplinary committee. At this point, the aim should not be to criticize but to detect and think of a solution.

Question the Situation

The conflicting employees or management must be questioned once again. The focal point should be on the following:

- Apportioned task

- Individual objectives

- Personal interest

- Individual recognition in the organization

- Personal clashes

- Initial discord

- The skillfulness of individual(s) for such task

The problem is likely to have a root in any of the above things. Get the involved parties to see their errors and make no mistake of supporting either party's personal interests or individual opinions. Do not be judgmental and avoid saying things that threaten the skillfulness of such individuals.

Demand Suggestions

Most organizations skip this stage of conflict management. The suggestions here must be those of the opposition. However, it does not mean HRM or management should implement their suggestions because it may end up not being favorable to both sides. However, requiring input from various sides shows a sense of commitment to resolution. Additionally, allowing either party to propose potential resolutions builds the integrity and trust that each party has in the process. Oftentimes, conflict arises because one party does not believe that the other party values their opinion or has listened to them with the intent of understanding. This calms the parties' defenses as they are allowed to express their discord and possible solutions. Strategists or human resource persons should be clear to explain that although suggestions are being taken, there is no guarantee that a particular suggestion would be implemented.

Review the Cause

Reviewing the sorted problem may or may not be done by a team of strategists. However, it is ideal to run this as a team of strategists in order for a more promising idea to be generated. While reviewing, there should be exceptional attention paid to the causes of the conflict rather than a solution. The reason is that knowing the problem leads to a solution. For example, sorting a conflict between two individuals with different objectives towards a similar objective would require that either both individuals be relieved of the task or both provided with specific duties in that same task. Further, knowing the cause will undoubtedly allow strategists to ultimately form solutions that proactively prevent further occurrences of the same or similar nature.

Implement

Implementing a resolution is the easiest of the tasks. This takes place either when both parties may have been relieved of the task causing the conflict or replaced. Whether a new individual or a team is introduced or initial parties are retained, the new strategy is what should be implemented. Implementing an old strategy with a new team may work, but the chances that the initial cause of the conflict will arise again is 50/50. The chances are neither promising nor worth a trial without sharp scrutiny and study of the newly tasked individual(s).

Monitor the New Policy and Make Amends

There must be a follow up of the new planned strategy. Keep an eye on the new policy and the individuals working with it.

Chapter Summary

◆ Conflict management is a reactive measure that helps to identify the source of a problem and identify a solution.

◆ Conflict is classified based on result, involvement, scope, or strategy. Each of these classes of conflict requires a particular approach in any attempt to resolve.

◆ Conflict management approaches include competing, accommodating, avoiding, collaborating, and compromising.

◆ Conflict arises from certain factors and could easily be resolved by employing certain resolution practices such as sourcing for cause, invitation of conflicting parties, questioning the situation, reviewing the cause, implementation of a plan and monitoring the implementation.

Quiz 5

1. Conflict can arise between any of the following [select all that apply]:

   a. The employer

   b. Management

   c. Employees

   d. Customers

2. What are some universally accepted approaches to conflict management?

   a. Competing, Assigning wrong duty, Assigning a team to source for cause, Questioning the situation

   b. Competing, Accommodating, Avoiding, Collaborating, & Compromising

   c. Competing, Termination, Implementing, inviting conflicting parties to discuss

   d. Competing, Acclimating, Avoiding, Communicating, & Compromising

3. Which of the following is not a difficulty that may arise due to conflict?

   a. Low productivity

   b. Increased productivity

   c. Weak communication

   d. Underperformance

4. Conflict is completely avoidable with the appropriate planning and strategies, and in most organizations will never occur. [True or False].

   a. True

   b. False

5. Molly and Pam are co-workers. They have always worked together on teams. During one of their team meetings, Molly expressed that she could no longer work with Pam because they didn't see eye-to-eye. Management was also present during the team meeting. It is evident that Molly and Pam are involved in a conflict. Based on the various classifications of conflict and the information provided which type is most evident?

   a. Value conflict

   b. Relationship conflict

   c. Task conflict

   d. Intrapersonal conflict

Solutions to the above questions can be downloaded from the **Online Resources** *section of this book on*
www.vibrantpublishers.com

This page is intentionally left blank

Chapter 6

Payroll And Compensation

T he focus for this chapter is payroll and compensation. It provides a broad introduction to the concepts the relevance they have in an organization.

Readers should be able to determine the following upon completing the chapter:

- Different payroll methods

- Various types of payroll systems

- Types of compensation practiced universally by different organizations

- The strategic plan behind implementing a working payroll and compensation plan in a company

- How payroll and compensation benefit the competence level of a company

- The various forms of compensation practiced universally by organizations

Payroll could be characterized by two definitions or functions. The first is that it is simply a collection of staff-workers alongside their salaries. It lists out the staff in an organization and also lists out the salary or wages. The amount of money paid either daily, weekly, or monthly, which is the salary or wage that may have been agreed during negotiations. That is, either a company pays what is in line with their policy or what an individual requires. The second is that payroll refers to the Human Resource Management tasked with the responsibility of administering and distributing money to the employees of an organization. Apart from this, Human Resource Management also determines what pay fits a job role or an employee.

Compensation, on the other hand, is a different terminology. It is merely an added benefit and may always come as a reparation, brilliance in performance, as a reward, or as payment for relief. It has nothing to do with salary and is often not negotiated as salary and wages unless it is a fixed compensation. Moreover, compensation is not something being debated about. It could be willful on the grounds of merit or worthiness. Compensation can be classified as a reward. As a reward, it is a suitable method of convincing a highly skilled employee to stay committed and loyal to the organization

Placing these two terms as concepts side by side, it suffices to say that the most necessary of the two is payroll. Compensation, however, can be necessary when it is fixed and not a variable. A variable compensation does not require a group of human resource managers to strike a strategic plan aimed at generating the right decision, but a fixed compensation does. Compensation, in general, requires reviews of some sort and may or may not be uncalled-for. On the other hand, when a seasoned payment (wages or salary) exceeds agreements without the knowledge of the employee, it is believed to be a compensation. This is so because the employee is not initially aware of the additional payments made.

It is a good practice for organizations to have a vibrant Human Resource Management department. The department should be able to control, administer, determine, and decide on an effective payroll structure. It must be such that it does not only agree with the unique policies of the organization but that it is capable of engineering the functionality of both the employees and the organization.

6.1 Concept of Payroll and Compensation

The concept of payroll is a little broader than it appears. Conventionally, it is known in any organization to either be the enlisted and attributed pay to be made to employees or as the Human Resource Management team that administers the payment. Payroll is practically what lures highly-skilled hands and brains. Moreover, since it refers to salaries and wages, it has a standardized level that regulatorily cannot be decreased or exceeded unless on agreement. Further, salary or wages, when not paid up to what the working conditions entail, become a legally noncompliant act that may result in costly payouts for any organization.

Methods of Payroll

Wages: This method of payroll is commonly practiced in organizations situated in developed countries. It comes with several advantages for the employee, such as not working beyond the agreed time. Also, employers would not prefer to keep hourly paid staff for an extended time as it will require more money to be paid to compensate for the additional hours.

Salary: This salary method is prevalent in developing and under-developing countries. It is a cheaper method than the wages payroll method, and the pay is usually not significant, in most cases. It may not be the best, but some employees definitely love this as a lump sum would be paid at once rather than a broken pay.

Commission: This method, unlike the salary and wages method, does not tie down an individual to a company. It is often contractual and packages lots of disadvantages. One such disadvantage is job security, which is seldom guaranteed.

Types of Payroll Systems

There are primarily four types of payroll systems. They include:

Internal Payroll System

Here, payments are managed within the organization by an individual or a group of workers. The individual or group is tasked with keeping records, and this may be done either manually or electronically. It is best practiced in smaller organizations.

External Payroll System

This is the opposite of the internal payroll system. An organization does not have full control wages and salary management for its employees. The external body is usually a licensed or authorized agency that takes an agreed percentage at the time of making payments. The chances that salary payment will become problematic is very low in this system.

Payroll Professional

A professional may be hired to overlook the employees' payments in an organization. He functions as an external body unless he is initially part of the company. Most organizations with an average number of employees practice this system.

Managerial Electronic System

This can also be called machine management. The accuracy of this system is high. However, humans are still required to maintain the servers, review, and modify the system from time to time.

As earlier stated, compensation could be a benefit or reparation. It defines or compliments an action. It is not automatically necessary, and it is not subject to any jurisdictional regulatory system. The rule of compliance does not overly cover the scope of compensation in an organization. However, a recent study identified aspects such as 'reparation' where it is necessary to compensate an employee. Thus, this makes compensation somewhat essential for employees, especially when it is a fixed compensation. Also, it will be unsound for any organization to fail to compensate staff, especially whose uncertain fate occurs within the company. Cases of injury are very rampant in manufacturing industries, and as such, compensation is often duly paid to such employees for treatment.

Types of Compensations

Fixed

This acts like wages and salaries. However, it is not an absolute salary in the sense that it only compensates a duty or responsibility, which could be only for that particular business period. Fixed compensation may be non-monetary, direct, or indirect compensation.

Variable

Only an organization may decide to offer variable compensation. Any regulatory law of jurisdiction does not compel it. A variable compensation may also be non-monetary, direct, or indirect compensation.

In general, the scope of compensation is to compliment an employee for something that may or may not be part of the job. For some companies practicing variable compensation is a trick-shot towards encouraging an employee to be committed. It is also a means to make sure an employee's contributions are well-recognized.

6.2 Aims and Objectives of Compensation

Every organization wants to reap the best results from their employees. As such, compensating their efforts is one of the many strategic approaches to do so. It is not necessary to dole out variable compensation, whether non-monetary, direct, or indirect. However, it is necessary to dole out compensation when it is fixed. This is because fixed compensation functions like a salary or wages.

For Keith Davies (1984), *"Compensation is what employees receive in exchange for their contribution to the organization."* Although Davies' definition does not emphatically state what type of compensation, it is clear that it will either be on the grounds of necessity or freewill from the organization.

Here are a few aims and objectives of compensation:

Retention of Skilled Employees

There are times when employees feel they should abandon a particular job for something better. To think of it, such employees are usually highly skilled employees who feel unappreciated for their performances and contributions. As a strategy, the introduction of compensation convinces such an employee that the organization is very well aware of his presence and contributions. The sort of category of compensation that applies here is variable compensation. It may come as a non-monetary compensation like a car gift, promotion, or work-leave, for example. It may also be direct or indirect compensation. An employee with plans to look away from the company may reconsider extending the duration such that he or she has been convinced of better treatment.

A Tool to Encourage Commitment

Most employees need encouragement to maintain productivity. When there is no form of encouraging strategy, such employees feel discouraged and dwindle in efficiency. The entire factors associated with the employee will witness a rapid and steady decline, which may or may not be noticeable in an organization. When compensation is introduced, such an employee's morale is boosted. Compensating employees is like a golden rope. It tempts an employee to willingly tie-down themselves for the sake of the company. The concept makes it possible for staff to feel pride for the company.

Minimize Expenses

A company that practices fixed compensation tends to be on the winning side. With such practice, a company can decide whom to pay a certain amount. Whereas, this is not so possible with salaried staff who earn at almost an equal margin. Moreover, a staff of fixed compensation is not so bound by regulatory laws as the company might relieve them at any point in time. In short, several top organizations practice this standard, especially when there is a vacancy that requires short-termed responsibility.

Regulatory Compliance

The laws of some jurisdictions state that employees must be rewarded for exceptional performances. This, however, is not as serious as several other regulatory rules that invoice fairness. But then, working terms that include fixed compensations are part of the regulatory guidelines. Fairness policies should not be policies begged for but practiced such that deserving employees get compensated duly. This may mean a bit more expenses, but it aids in boosting employee performance, and this is an objective of compensation.

Encourage Self-Discipline Among Employees

It is very rampant for employees to bring in the ideology of red tape, especially in organizations where there is zero employee discipline. The red tape ideology is mostly prevailing in government organizations but has recently extended to private organizations. Employees tend to practice this with a supporting belief that the organization is, after all, doing nothing to encourage their performance.

6.3 Benefits of Compensation

Compensating staff has benefits that stretch from emotional to physical aspects. These aspects each have roles to fill for the growth of the company. Besides, compensation is something that every employee should be entitled to for effectiveness.

Some scholars have pronounced their thoughts on the concept of compensation, and one such is Edwin's thought. Edwin Flippo (1980) speculates, *"The function of compensation is defined as the adequate and equitable remuneration of personnel for their contributions to the organizational objectives."* Although Edwin's definition is not broad enough, a lot could be extracted from the definition. As an employer, one of the many targets is to attain a certain level of success. Such being the case, strategies like employee compensation is required to prevail in the business. Compensation provides several benefits. These benefits apply to both employees and employers.

For employees, the benefits include:

- An opportunity to tour a preferred destination
- Promotion
- Managerial role
- Additional incentives
- An award of excellence

The primary benefits for organizations include rapid employee development, staff loyalty and commitment, retention of highly-skilled minds, and absolute control of the system.

Rapid Employee Development

Compensation facilitates employees' development at a faster pace. Whether the compensation type is variable or fixed, the beneficial implication is that it encourages employee development. An individual who is newly employed or that has to adapt to work changes needs development for better and productive performance. Once compensation is duly or unduly in place, such an individual would have to rethink what he or she is doing. The employee may contend, *"It looks like someone values what I am doing, I should do better."* For quicker development, he might resort to undergoing online courses and learning more about the system to invent new impactful ideas.

Staff Loyalty and Commitment

An employee may love the job, but that does not mean they are loyal and committed. A strategic plan aimed at unleashing this part of the employee must be put in place. One such plan, as often mentioned in this section, is 'compensation.' It convinces an employee of the admiration an organization has towards their performances. Nothing beats loyalty, and this should be the gift to boost yield.

Retention of Highly-Skilled Minds

An organization of 10 staff can perform better or remain more competitively sound than an organization of 40. There is no magic in this, and if there is, then 'skillfulness' is the magic. The objective of recruitment is not to simply accept everyone who applies for a position within the organization. Instead, the idea is to be selective and to pick minds capable of producing quality results in the company. Compensation, thus, makes it possible for employees of high standards to be retained in an organization. Human Resource Management should be very attentive to this aspect of human management as the exit of a star employee may cost an organization's performance to suffer.

Absolute Control of the Monetary System

Absolute control over the monetary system is particularly applicable to agreed-upon working conditions based on fixed compensation. Recall that a fixed compensation may be salary as well as wages. However, in most instances, they do not serve as salaries since the job in place is often indentured (i.e., on a contractual basis). How does this provide monetary control to employers? It is what several organizations practice to cut the cost of recruiting the wrong minds and an impotently expensive workforce.

6.4 Payroll Strategies

The strategy applies in several faculties of human resource management. Without a well-planned strategy, it will be somewhat difficult to get over outstanding and unpromising circumstances. In the case of payroll, improper payroll management might cause an organization to lose its competitive prowess or even go bankrupt. Extensively, there will be problems with poor ascertainable payment scales. In such cases, an organization would either be overpaying or underpaying a workforce. Either way, none of it is positively impactful until a redress.

Payroll may be managed and computed manually or automatically. For several small organizations, a manual system is preferred, but a manual system will not sit well with a large. Large organizations operating manual processing may face accountability problems. That notwithstanding, whether manual or automatic, without a proper strategic plan, it will be meaningless. Consider the below-screened strategy to achieve perfect payroll management.

Employ Orderly Approaches

The first attempt towards having effective payroll management relies on orderliness. The standard required is a hierarchical slope from the top category to the least. What determines a payroll control system lies in how the entire organization positions responsibilities. An organization with mixed responsibilities and lack of specialty will result in a disorder that will as well affect payroll management. To fix the issue, a review and a redress must be made. Ensure that there is an organized system of categorized employees. They should each have a task to their name, and there must be a review of staff qualification as well as duty type.

Pick a Payroll Management System

The basic payroll management systems include internal systems, external systems, professional personnel systems, and automatic or electronic systems. Internal, external, and professional management may as well decide to operate a manual or electronic method that depends on the nature of the organization. It may be a bit tricky sorting out a working system at first. However, understanding the present nature of the organization and the employees should make it easier. Moreover, abide by the managerial principles by allowing this at the mercy of Human Resource Management for a payroll system that will work for the organization.

Be Direct

A fathomable process may appear easy and, at the same time, not too secure. However, it works. Aspirations may be for things to take an absurd style, but, in truth, it has the potential to affect the overall performance of the company. If there is an already-in-place department in charge of payroll, clearly define aspirations and allow them the liberty to engage in the task as professionals, even though they may not be professionals. Encourage them to take online courses for more rapid intellectual development, which would be helpful in the system.

Outsource Payroll Management

The ideology behind outsourcing is an attempt to redress difficulties in payroll management. Basically, it looks to cut off internal loads on employees tasked with payroll management. Instead of waggling and possibly negatively meandering with the system, source for a certified alternative to handle the processes. Several agencies and individual professionals specialize solely in the payroll management of an organization. Either of these bodies would be necessary if the process becomes stagnant. Their presence will mean relief and a fuller concentration on the productive aspect of the company.

Supervise the New Method

Once satisfied with a payroll system that has potential, introduce it to the organization. Find out the policies, compare the policies with those of the organization as well as those of the regulatory system, and allow it in. If the conditions are not favorable, do not force it on the organization as doing so would cause more harm than good.

6.5 Diverse Forms of Compensation

The forms of compensation may be direct or indirect. An employee may have control over compensation if it is a fixed direct type of compensation. On the other hand, indirect compensation often comes as a freewill from a company. The company may or may not decide to dole out, such as remuneration.

Figure 6.1

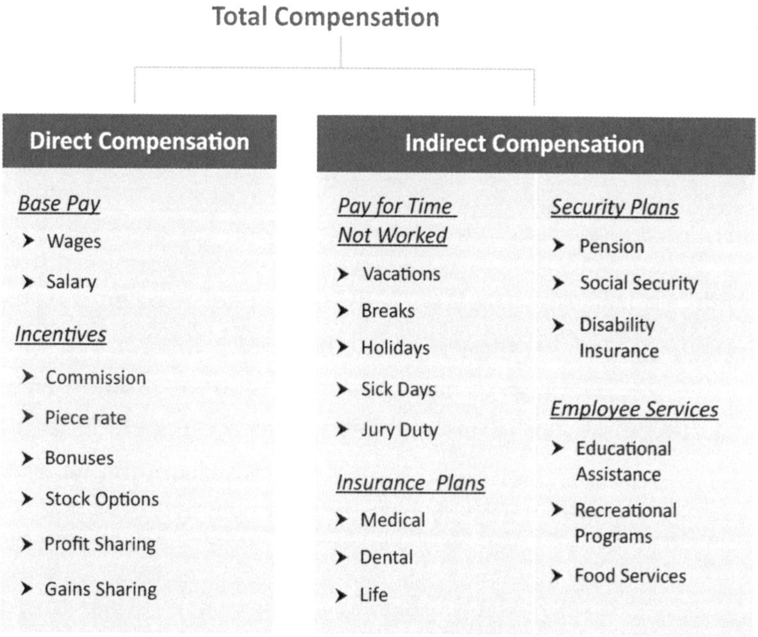

Total Compensation

Direct Compensation	Indirect Compensation	
Base Pay	*Pay for Time Not Worked*	*Security Plans*
➤ Wages	➤ Vacations	➤ Pension
➤ Salary	➤ Breaks	➤ Social Security
Incentives	➤ Holidays	➤ Disability Insurance
➤ Commission	➤ Sick Days	
➤ Piece rate	➤ Jury Duty	*Employee Services*
➤ Bonuses		➤ Educational Assistance
➤ Stock Options	*Insurance Plans*	➤ Recreational Programs
➤ Profit Sharing	➤ Medical	
➤ Gains Sharing	➤ Dental	➤ Food Services
	➤ Life	

Direct

Direct compensation is such that comes in the form of cash. It can be a reward as well as a remuneration or earning. Being a reward or a remuneration, an employer may or may not be compelled to compensate and employee. In cases where it is fixed, then an employee is judicially compelled to clear the employee. Four types of direct compensation include salary, wages, commission, and fiscal bonuses.

Salary

An employee working on compensation as salary is tied to a fixed type of compensation. However, such agreements are often contractual and short-termed. Moreover, an employer may relieve an employee of this payroll at any point in time.

Wages

Unlike salary, compensation is fixed when it has been agreed upon by both employer and employee. If it is variable compensation, it suggests that such staff is full-time rather than a short-term employee. Variable wages are paid on the grounds of overtime work, additional jobs (outside working conditions), and a few other reasons.

Commissions

This sort of compensation is designed based on percentage. Here, an employer designs and decides on what a workforce will be paid. The workforce may be at liberty to negotiate, but this is not always the case. A workforce under this category is short-termed and may be relieved at any time by the employer.

Fiscal Bonus

Fiscal bonus is purely a freewill from an employer. It is an added incentive usually to motivate an employer to stay committed.

Indirect

These are nonmonetary compensations and are often variable compensations such that an employer is not compelled to give. Although an employer is not judicially compelled to compensate an employee on this note, it is necessary to encourage such an employer in several ways. Indirect forms of compensations include a promotion, free tour, non-fiscal gifts, and a few others.

Promotion

When there is compensation with promotion, it gives an employer a step or steps progress. Everyone loves to move one or more steps forward, and this is one of such ways to make an employee have a sense of belonging.

Tour

A company may decide to sponsor an employee on tour to a destination of choice. This also serves as leave for such an employee. On return, such an employee would want to keep his or her head high and attract such an opportunity once again. It is a great way to keep an employee's determination and skillfulness alive.

Non-fiscal Gift

This includes gifts such as a car, an apartment, and more. It is intended to give comfort to the employee and to motivate the employee to stay committed and disciplined in the job.

Chapter Summary

◆ Payroll is characterized by two definitions or functions: 1) a collection of staff-workers alongside their salaries, and 2) an HR task of administering and distributing money to the employees of an organization.

◆ Compensation may be an added benefit usually aimed at convincing or encouraging individuals or employees to perform better.

◆ The primary methods of compensation include wages, salaries, and compensation.

◆ The various types of payroll systems which include internal, external, payroll professional and electronic system each have a definitive impact on an organization.

◆ The payroll system practiced by an organization must fit its standard.

◆ Compensation provides several benefits to employees, but also provides benefits to the organization.

Quiz 6

1. Internal, External, payroll professional, and managerial electronic system are all types of:

   a. Payroll systems

   b. Management systems

   c. Accounting systems

   d. Communication systems

2. Which of the following is not considered a benefit of compensation to employees?

   a. Staff loyalty

   b. Excellence award

   c. A promotion

   d. A tour

3. Compensating employees helps to encourage _____.

   a. non-compliance

   b. turnover

   c. commitment

   d. overtime

4. **Salary, wages, compensation, and commission are all the same thing. [True or False].**

   a. True

   b. False

5. **Large organizations are more likely to prefer a(n) _____ payroll system over a(n) _____ system.**

   a. outsourced, automatic

   b. automatic, manual

   c. internal, manual

   d. manual, automatic

Solutions to the above questions can be downloaded from the **Online Resources** *section of this book on* **www.vibrantpublishers.com**

Chapter 7

Concept Of IT In HRM

Information Technology (IT) is a necessary construct in any organization.

Chapter seven highlights the following:

- The effect of IT on HRM

- Disadvantages of IT in HRM

- The relevance of IT in HRM and the need to employ IT systems in an organization

- Main challenges of IT in HRM

The need for technology in any organization should not be ignored. Although some fear that technology will promote the introduction of robots as a workforce, humans are still filling positions. Several organizations have admitted the importance of information technology (IT) as it aids in achieving goals near perfectly. Before now, the manual forms of operations made things difficult to accomplish. However, the basics of information technology, being automatic, present hefty and time-consuming tasks in an optimized and ordered manner.

It will conventionally take days, if not weeks, to sort out minor things like an updated regulatory policy for organizational compliance. However, the advertency of Human Resource Management to technology could fix this within minutes of going online and retrieving an updated regulatory policy data. Not only does the mode of retrieval appear easy, understanding the policy becomes easier as a human resource person may not have to contact the governing agencies in person for more enlightenment on specific policies.

Information Technology and HRM

Human Resource Management is tasked with responsibilities including employee development, recruitment of skilled employees, training, ensuring legal compliance, encouraging employees at work, formulating new policies, and more. All of these functions can now be rendered effortlessly with the aid of technology, which couples several predesigned instructions that make it easier for large tasks to be cut; needless to say, an aspect like payroll management in an organization. A larger percentage of organizations have switched to automatic or electronic payroll systems, which feature accuracy and transparency in accountability.

With the introduction of IT in Human Resource Management, there is now a 'responsibility shift.' Human Resource Management barely has to flip through pages to review employee performance and also do not pass through hassles to obtain updated regulatory policies and principles, which are then integrated into the managerial system of an organization. Instead of all these, management can make strategic planning a focal point to keep competition alive and healthy.

Disadvantage of IT in HRM

No study doubts the relevance of technology in Human Resource Management. However, there are doubts by a few studies on the adverse effects of technology. For instance, an organization of 80 employees is estimated to have at least one human resource person. Going by this estimate, in an organization of 150 employees, the number will increase to at least two human resource persons, and this will continue to increase. Usually, larger organizations should have a number of human resource persons enough to be called a team of strategists. However, technology cuts down the number by more than half as only a few persons can manage a large group with the proper technology. Here are the primary disadvantages of IT in HRM.

- Risk of unemployment of HR professionals

- A smaller number of human resource persons in an organization

- Unexpected employee data breach/crash

- Lazy mindedness of Human Resource Management

- Over-dependence on machines

This extends to employees in an organization. The impact, just as in Human Resource Management, negatively affects employees. Rather than being judged by humans, employees risk being judged or assessed by machines, which will not be effective in the emotional aspect. Some of the notable effects on technology on employees include unemployment, lesser recognition, incorrect/undefining scores from machines, and a few more to mention. All in all, depending on how technology is managed in an organization, it makes an excellent addition to the company.

7.1 Importance of IT in HRM

The mention of technology in Human Resource Management as a means for flexibility draws immediate attention. A difficult task can be tiring no matter the pay involved, but when the job is flexible, one would want to do more. This is the general benefit of technology in Human Resource Management that many human resource persons find alluring.

Technology gives management a sense of swiftness. It keeps records of activities, and most advantageous, it makes them easily accessible. In every computer software, there is a 'search' feature provided. This feature makes it easier to quickly access a given file no matter its location. Sometimes it is necessary to instruct a computer on what result to present. Comparing this to a non-technology-based Human Resource Management, searching for a particular file would require flipping through pages which consumes time and energy.

Technology is very relevant, although it has a few glitches. Let's glance through the central importance of technology in HRM that help to build and develop an organization towards success.

Absolute Focus on Management

With technology, the focal point of Human Resource Management will be on strategic planning. Recall that the relevance of HR is essentially on management. However, it is often tricky as the HR department would have to be attentive to all aspects of the company at the same time. With technology, the workload is decreasing as Human Resource Management tends to focus more on strategic planning rather than an every-time problem-solving technique. Simply, this means that the managerial team of an organization will have to worry less about several other things and focus more on the technical area of development.

Automatically Grade Employees

Performance scorecards are being introduced in several organizations as a means of monitoring and reviewing employee performance. HR sets up these systems and installs each on the appropriate systems in the organization. It could as well include employee work computers. Some companies anonymously install these to monitor the activities of employees in order to know who is being committed and who is not. This can also be termed an electronic appraisal.

Flexibility, Speed, and Accuracy

This was earlier mentioned as the essential scope of technology. Human Resource Management has substantial flexibility. With technology, there is flexibility in all ramifications of management, including the thinking aspect. How is IT relevant in thinking? It merely provides easy access to the required stats/updates for effective decisions. Moreover, HR persons do not require file stacks to store data used in running the organization.

With speed, there is a rapid progression in the business. The speed here includes even the decision-making process. With technology, this is not an unsolvable difficulty. For instance, it provides room for a comprehensive analysis of the market speedily, thereby ensuring better risk management. It helps to stay abreast of market changes and to be able to formulate new strategies that will either increase the company's competitive prowess or maintain its level.

Accountability

Operating on a manual standard is likely to make the accounting task difficult and incomprehensible. Managing payrolls in a noncomputerized way will lead to inaccurate records and will cause confusion. This is not the case when technology is involved because of the calculative ability is holds. A simple coding will be able to collect data, compile, sum up, and present a perfect result that can be accounted for. For this to be the case in an organization, such an organization must outsource for payroll systems like hiring an external payroll agency or professional to overlook the process of employee salaries and wages. IT goes as far as helping to determine the worth of a recruit in an organization correctly.

7.2 Challenges Faced by IT in HRM

It is necessary to understand the significant technology loopholes to understand better how to manage situations when the need arises. Despite the relevance of technology in the business system, some downsides must not be overlooked for effectiveness.

Anything related to technology in an organization is subject to the legal and regulatory laws of a jurisdiction. For example, the 1989 Electricity at Work Regulations compels organizations to managerial principles that could expel or minimize the electric hazards that have harmful effects on the environment. Also, the Gas Safety Regulations 1998 presses on the effectiveness of employing specific measures that could prevent disastrous incidents, which could lead to the loss of lives. Failure to conform to these principles, as always mentioned, attracts punishments, which may be monetary charges, a suspension/ban, long judicial processes, as well as facing certain limitations.

This said, here are the three primary challenges faced by IT in Human Resource Management.

Security

Once there is an integration of technology in an organization, attacks begin to fly in. The worst scenario is when a said organization is entirely wireless. Such will require a high level of wireless security as hackers will attempt to install malware on the connections to gain access to the web system of the company. Also, every data entry that is utilized in an organization is risky as there may be trojans designed to travel with such data. Meanwhile, the present height of competitiveness among competitors is such that competitors hire programmers to design malware for unwarranted access to a fellow competitor's web base. This is done in a bid to monitor competitor's progress and changes in order to plan a strategy that performs better and remains at the top level of the competition.

Data Loss

The loss of data is a rampant problem with technology. Whether data is saved online or offline, there are chances that a breach might be initiated, and data would either be stolen or crashed. As a case study, Yahoo suffered a breach in 2013, which affected about 3 billion accounts and meant a significant loss to the company. Now, what was supposed to serve as a medium for quick communication became a huge problem. This applies the same to Human Resource Management, who risks losing an employee and organizational data to hackers. Since this does not comply with the standards of individual data security, not only would losses be suffered but also legal charges for noncompliance with data security.

Cost of Management

The integration of technology in Human Resource Management is not very cost-effective. Management would have to hire or pay professionals to run checks on the system for security constantly. The cost of securing the base from hacks does not come cheap; however, it is better to settle the cost of securing data rather than lose them. Software preferred for managing an organization's web system must be premium, and this means paying out a few bucks for subscriptions either on a monthly or yearly basis.

7.3 IT Applications in HRM

The introduction of technology in Human Resource Management has altered the entire managerial processes. For example, instead of human resource persons focusing on the general management of an organization, technology aids in shifting focus to strategic management, which is more like a proactive problem solver. The importance of technology applies to both employees and management. Employees have taken advantage of the presence of technology to handle jobs with ease and effectiveness. This is the case when employees have to work from home as well as give feedback to the management from wherever.

Management has introduced the aspect of information technology to the system for swifter operations. Such includes employee rate cards, easy regulatory and compliance policy updates, recruiting the best individuals, and timely job delivery from employees. Somehow, technology has curbed the unpromising distantness between employees and employers. As an employer today, it is effortless to connect with any employee of your choice. A simple ping from your home or office, and the employee would be notified. Also, discussing bothersome issues could take place from the bedroom. Needless to mention the advanced meeting concepts presently practiced in larger organizations whereby there is no physical presence.

There is no longer a need to await a report from market spies as a few clicks on the internet reveal accurate data and present the condition of the market. Employee self-development is now easier than ever with several tools provided by IT. For example, websites are offering free and paid online courses and tutorials – written and visual. What an employee requires is a simple data connection and software like YouTube and Udemy. There are a series of video tutorials on YouTube and online paid and free courses on Udemy. An employee who finds time for any of these will likely develop and perform ten times better than a redundant employee. It is also the duty of Human Resource Management to encourage employees to practice these sorts of self-trainings in order to match up with the competition.

Frankly, there have been many positives accompanying the introduction of technology to business organizations. There are now instances where employees deliver for daily jobs with minor taps and clicks on their iPads and laptops. Are the clients left out? Not at all. Clients are not left out; rather, they continue to enjoy the innovativeness of HR persons in the development of better standards and increased efficiencies.

Chapter Summary

◆ It is essential to understand the framework of IT in HRM.

◆ IT in HRM could sometimes be defective and this often results from either improper management strategies or natural cause. The defection is a natural cause in the sense that programs fail or malfunction.

◆ Despite the downside of IT in HRM, it is an important aspect of a company.

◆ Technology has curbed the unpromising distantness between employees and employers.

◆ Clients also enjoy the innovativeness that IT contributes to an organization's development and productivity.

Quiz 7

1. With technology in place, HRM can focus more on _____.

   a. recruiting

   b. payroll

   c. strategic planning

   d. compliance

2. Which of the following is **not** considered a disadvantage of IT in HRM?

   a. A risk of being judged or assessed by machines

   b. Risk of unemployment of HR professionals

   c. Lazy mindedness of Human Resource Management

   d. Increased accuracy and transparency in accountability

3. Which of the following are challenges faced by IT in HRM [select all that apply]?

   a. cost of managing technology

   b. security

   c. accountability

   d. loss of data

4. **Hackers may attempt to install malware to gain access to systems. One reason competitors would also do this is to:**

   a. assist the competitor with a competitive advantage

   b. engage in file sharing to build a stronger force against larger companies

   c. monitor a competitor's progress and changes

   d. decrease the likeliness of viruses and data loss

5. **Legal charges could be assessed for failing to comply with data security requirements [True or False].**

   a. True

   b. False

*Solutions to the above questions can be downloaded from the **Online Resources** section of this book on* **www.vibrantpublishers.com**

This page is intentionally left blank

Chapter 8

IT Platforms In HRM: HRMS v/s HRIS v/s HCM

C hapter eight discusses and compares different IT platforms.

It focusses on the following:

- Three IT platforms prominent in Human Resource Management: HRMS, HRIS and HCM

- The similarities and differences between the three identified IT platforms.

- Features of HRMS, HRIS, and HCM.

Technology in Human Resource Management extends to several faculties, including Human Resource Management System (HRMS), Human Resource Information System (HRIS), and Human Capital Management (HCM). This covers every aspect of management in an organization and can be very effective when applied well. The concept of technology in Human Resource Management stretches to various faculties as well. It is a broad concept, as earlier mentioned, and thrives on the abilities of the individuals managing the technological processes. Most organizations with a dedicated resource management department still go on to delegate responsibilities to specific human persons.

Without proper planning and implementation of technology in any management, the managerial system will go bad, and the organization will be affected. The story will be the reverse if the relevance of technology is recognized and introduced to the system. With in-place technology, the chances that the system will diminish is low. This is so because the management will be spared attention to several facets of an organizational dealing while focusing on the formulation of more working strategies. For example, in terms of policy management, Human Resource Management does not have to dispatch a team or an individual to go and queue up in the court to learn and return with updates. The judicial system simply uploads the new data on the internet while the managerial department downloads reviews to ensure compliance, and updates the already existing policy.

There are three facets of resource management to be compared in this section and include HRMS, HRIS, and HCM. These anchors are in no way different. However, they are the components of Human Resource Management. In short, an intelligent HR department must split the management into these sorts of units.

HRMS could sometimes be interchangeably used with HRIS. However, these two systems differ. HRMS entirely manages workforce data, activities data, strategies, and plans of an organization. The system comprises entries that help to see through the organization and to keep track of relevant activities. It can also be the collection of data that defines an organization. This implies that the HRMS is the heart of an organization's information. Every human resource person may have to refer to this tool(s) in order to get a fuller glimpse of their duties.

HRIS is purely concerned with information. This technical tool houses relevant data such as company policy, mode of operation, staff details, company budgets, company target, and more. It is a subsystem of HRMS but differs in the sense that it is more concerned with information storage and retrieval. This is the most security-concerned tool due to its sensitivity.

The third in this study is Human Capital Management (HCM). HCM is equally an aspect of HRMS in HRM. HCM mostly relates to employee development. It is merely the search for a decent workforce referred to as human capital and the development as well as retention of such a workforce.

8.1 Human Resource Management System (HRMS)

HRMS has to do with the overall management of an organization, its workforce, and other parts. It directly concerns the employment of any available scientific, ordered, and straightforward principles in the running of the system. It could sometimes be referenced as Human Resource Information

(HRIS), but this will be delimiting its purpose. Unlike HRIS, HRMS encompasses every strategy, managerial skills, employee activities, payroll system, security functions, and employer target. It is believed by various organizations to be the way forward in management. As database management, it makes it easy and swift for data to be stored and retrieved at any time. HRMS can also be called an automated tool for management. The automatic tasks performed by this tool employers, employees, and management alike. With system integration, organizations can run specific tasks online at ease and with convenience. For example, employees in some organizations can apply for a leave or a break online without sending papers to the management. When this request arrives at the system, the system will automatically scan and grade the request. A response would then be passed to the employee notifying whether he or she is eligible.

A relatively short time ago, the processes involved in keeping records of employees were much more tedious. Organizations had to encounter loss of manually stored data, and sometimes this was lost due to natural disasters such as fire, flood, earthquake, and so much more. A proper HRMS has all of the relevant data backed up somewhere and such that any lost information can always be easily replaced or retrieved anywhere in the world.

Organizations love to work with the best skilled and committed minds. The first step is ensuring this feat is recruitment. The system helps to gather and recruit qualified individuals that can bring something to the table. HRMS is what every organization needs to remain active in every section of the business. Also, having the right individuals in this department matters. A less equipped human resource person finds it difficult to cope with the requirements. If the difficulty is high, even with technological resources, consider involving more individuals to strengthen up and boost results.

8.2 Human Resource Information System (HRIS)

The Human Resource Information System (HRIS) is a sub aspect of the HRMS. This aspect deals with the appropriation of information. This information is what an organization requires to plan its strategies and to keep track of its progress. Practically, it is the most sensitive aspect of HRM and sub aspect of HRMS. An organization requires information to operate in conformation with standards.

Extensively, HRIS is a tool that supports aspects of an organization such as policy compliance, merit for reward, fixed compensation payments, employee appraisal, employee request, activity data collection and management, activity progress, and reports.

HRIS encourages transparency. It also serves as a tool or software for the supervision, review, and processing of money-related activities.

The presence of the information system is scrapping the initial hectic calculations and difficult-to-grasp modes of keeping records. Moreover, the shift of responsibilities becomes more relaxed as the involved persons may not have to go through long but relevant tutoring processes. For example, in an organization where a new payroll assistant is recruited, it may take just a few days for the recruit to adapt to the system. How is this made easy with information management? It is simply done by providing the recruit with an already ordered data containing all monetary aspects of the organization. A staff name will appear alongside the earning, which, when summed up, is called payroll. In short, a recruit may likely do nothing as the system is designed to collect, compile, and report employee earnings automatically. In most advanced scenarios, the system can rate an employee on what may be referred to as a grade card. This card will enable the company to tell which employee performed best and which did not. The company may then decide to reward a high performing employee or invite and inform and find out why a particular employee is underperforming.

The most intriguing feature of this web-based system is that it is simple to install and run. It may not be simple to those who are not professionals in the field but definitely to professionals. An organization may have to hire professionals to design and set up the system in a way that will be easy for the human resource persons to work with for results.

HRIS suffers a few problems related to security. An organization must be alert to suspicious activities that may lead to data breaches. Sometimes, one's level of security protocols may not be enough for system management. As such, there should be a practice of proactive security maintenance. Two such include a frequent backup of organizational data. This includes employee's payroll, company policies, daily and monthly activities, subscription to premium security software, and hiring of the security management team to run checks on the system.

8.3 Human Capital Management (HCM)

This aspect more concisely has to do with the management of human capital. Sir William Arthur Lewis is recognized as the first economist to introduce the term 'human capital' to the management sphere. It refers to the objectives, formalities, strategies, and attempts made towards ensuring that employees receive the best beginning from encouragement, reward, compensations, recruitment of the best individuals, development, and retention of skillful employees.

HCM recognizes the importance of the workforce in an organization. The scope of HCM is to convince employees to be committed and loyal to the company. The scope of HCM also encourages organizations to be particularly attentive to the employees since they are productive minds. Without employees, every other resource will be useless. An organization cannot exist without a workforce that drives it to success. The various activities that take place in any organization have an objective, which is usually to acquire a competitive prowess and utilize it to have a competitive advantage over competitors.

Employees or human capital also have a role when it comes to human capital management. Their role is such that their activities must comply with the internal policies of the organization and that they perform up to the requirements or work in compliance with the job terms initially agreed upon. Two essential instances should not be ignored when dealing with human capital. The first is that when the attempts to train and develop an employee do not yield desired results, such an employee should be relieved of the duty. Allowing such an employee to continue with such duty may lead to a break that affects all angles of the organization.

Secondly, an unhappy employee must not be forced to stay in an organization. Although the scope of HCM encourages attention and compensation of human capital, it undoubtedly argues against the retention of unwilling employees. This could be poisonous and relatively dangerous to the growth of the organization.

Figure 8.1

HRIS	HCM	HRMS
➤ Policy Compliance	➤ Encouragement	➤ Encompasses Every Strategy
➤ Merit For Reward	➤ Reward	➤ Managerial Skills
➤ Fixed Compensation Payments	➤ Compensations	➤ Employee Activities
➤ Employee Appraisal	➤ Recruitment of The Best Individuals	➤ Payroll System
➤ Employee Request	➤ Development	➤ Security Functions
➤ Activity Data Collection and Management	➤ Retention of Skillful Employees	➤ Employer Target
➤ Activity Progress		
➤ Reports		

8.4 Similarities Between HRMS, HRIS, and HCM

HRMS, HRIS, and HCM are often identified as similar concepts. This is not far from correct, as there are notable similarities between them. It is also the sameness of these three concepts that make it almost difficult for organizations to decide on which to practice or make a focal point. The general objective that connects these concepts is that they are structured towards the achievement of a planned goal. This objective is where we derive the various similar objectives, notable as an outcome for integrating these concepts in an organization.

The basic similarities between HRMS, HRIS, and HCM are as follows:

Employee Development

The concepts mentioned above prompt a discussion of employee development. HRMS, HRIS, and HCM recognize the role of human capital in any organization. As such, the concepts promote employee development since an employee is regarded as the 'heart of production.' Without employees, an organization will not be able to set a target. Even when such an organization sets a target, it will lack vitality.

Scientific Measures

Proper management undergoes a series of trials and errors. This happens scientifically after a well-planned and craftily designed idea towards achieving success. These management concepts involve well-defined scientific processes for results. For example, HCM, which deals purely with employee management, takes time to chisel out and decide upon. Being that it involves individual recruitment, encouragement, development, and training, the responsible human resource person or persons would have to strike out tested ideas that are methodically developed to sort employee difficulties at any angle.

Strategies to Reach an Organizational Goal

The general aim of management is to develop or build an

organization towards success. Neither of these three concepts works without basis. That is, there is always a desired achievement that triggers the employment of these managerial concepts. To attain the goal, strategies including employee training, retention of skilled workers, recruitment of brilliant individuals, and others must be implemented.

Require the Integration of Technology

Practically, HRMS, HRIS, and HCM are technology-based concepts. Although either of these concepts can be manually functional, it is not recommendable to operate the system manually in this industrial age, especially when the number of employees is substantial. Technology in these management systems makes the workflow swift. It ensures accuracy and promotes high yields. Over 80% of organizations - small and large, have adopted electronic approaches towards management. The result from these organizations have been promising, and the number grows yearly, which means that several establishments worldwide have encountered the need to rely on technology by using available software and hardware in the organization.

Run by a Professional or a Group

Neither of these systems can run without personnel. There must be an employed or hired professional or professionals to overlook the system, review, modify, and implement relevant changes.

Costly to Maintain

Running these systems comes with a cost. However, these costs are most often worth it. Some costs include the renewal of data connection, payment for system management, a monthly or yearly subscription to premium security services, and others. Without spending to maintain the processes and make regular updates, the system may malfunction.

8.5 Differences Between HRMS, HRIS, and HCM

In a general sense, these systems bear some sort of sameness but have significant differences. Of all three systems, the most identical systems are HRMS and HRIS. This is because both systems have to do with the direct management of human and nonhuman resources relating to an organization. HCM, on the other hand, refers to human capital, and the system rallies solely around the development of employees or workforce.

Traditionally, the concept of HRM is a single concept. HRMS, HRIS, and HCM are just systems under the concept of HRM that make organizational management have focal points. That is, each system has its focal point, which better describes its purpose in human resource management. Let us identify the fundamental contrasts that exist between HRMS, HRIS, and HCM management systems.

Features of HRMS

Basically, HRMS comprises the features in HRIS and HCM. It thus suffices to say that HRMS is a collection of both HRIS and HCM. In essence, there is no exceptional feature that differs HRMS from its counterparts, and this makes it the ideal system. However, it is not just an ideal system but a complex type. It requires double the requirements for HRIS and HCM. The basic features of HRMS include the following:

Payroll management

HRMS manages employees' salaries, automates direct bank deposits, and deducts taxes where necessary. It could sometimes be programmed to add monetary incentives to employees with an excellent scorecard.

Labor Management

HRMS is capable of noting employee activities either on a daily, weekly, or monthly basis. It compiles and reports the compilation to management who scrutinizes the report and makes subsequent amends where necessary.

Time Management

It also calculates labor or working hours and could make predictions as well as accurately schedule a time for certain activities to take place.

Recruitment

The system can schedule a time to disseminate job postings to job boards coupled with a clear description of the job. It possesses a scoring system that helps to identify the best candidate for the job.

Features of HRIS

HRIS is not as broad as HRMS; however, the system is almost identical to HRMS.

The basic features of HRIS include the following:

Employee Development

HRIS is designed to aid rapid employee development. It makes readily available the relevant data required by organizations to review periodic employee data for appraisals that may result in either a reward or a proposal for training programs. The system here is based on digits or points. For every activity period, the system calculates and reports the performance score of an employee. Given that no employee fancies being the least rated, every employee will attempt to cheat the system or obtain points great enough to beat those of others. As such, they improvise mediums to fix job requirements and become proactively engaged in tutorials, online and offline, that makes them the betters in the role for recognition and possible variable compensation.

DIY Portal

The system provides a medium for every member of an organization to modify and update their profile. With this, an employee does not have to go through any physical paperwork entry to achieve the feat. It brings about swiftness in the process flow of change actions

Employee and Management Records

All employees and management records are safely stored for easy retrieval and reference.

Recruitment

HRIS plays a role in recruitment processes. It could be programmed to make vacant positions readily available for job seekers who meet the requirements.

Features of HCM

HCM is synonymous with 'human capital.' It is more concerned with employee development to boost the competitive advantage of an organization. Here are the basic features of HCM in management.

Employee Training/Talent Management

It encourages employee development by issuing training measures. It helps to identify talents and also shifts an employee to the right duty.

Employee Compensation

HCM keeps track of employee activities and calculates variable rewards as well as fixed rewards. It keeps track of the payment and may suggest what an individual deserves owing to the completed task.

Score Card and Salary Plan

It scores individuals and forwards the report to the management for employee appraisal. It also determines what salary or wages an individual deserves. The system equally determines what recruits in an organization deserve to earn.

Access to Internal Policies

Employees have access to updated organizational policies and work in conformation to the stated policies. An employee may also submit comments, suggestions, or concerns about a stated policy or the entire policy.

Chapter Summary

◆ An HR department must split the management into three facets.

◆ Although these platforms are categorized differently, there are still notable similarities existing between them.

◆ There are fundamental similarities between HRMS, HRIS and HCM, which include: employee development, scientific measures, strategies to reach goals, technology integration, how the system is operated, and maintenance cost.

Quiz 8

1. The following are similarities between HRMS, HRIS and HCM [select all that apply].

   a. Employee development

   b. Scientific measures

   c. Strategies to reach a goal

   d. Require IT integration

   e. Run by a professional or group

   f. Costly to maintain

   g. None of the above

2. The _____ system is a tool that supports aspects of an organization such as policy compliance, merit for reward, fixed compensation payments, employee appraisal, employee request, activity data collection and management, activity progress, and reports.

   a. HRMS

   b. HRIS

   c. HCM

   d. IT

3. The _____ system has to do with the overall management of an organization, its workforce, and other parts. It directly concerns the employment of any available scientific, ordered, and straightforward principles in the running of the system.

   a. HRMS

   b. HRIS

   c. HCM

   d. IT

4. The _____ comprises the features in _____ and _____. Therefore, is a collection of the other two systems.

   a. HRIS, HCM, HRMS

   b. HCM, HRIS, HRMS

   c. HRMS, HRIS, HCM

   d. IT, HRMS, HRIS

5. **Which of the following is not a feature of one of the IT platforms, HRIS, HCM, or HRMS?**

   a. Procurement management

   b. Payroll management

   c. Employee development

   d. Recruitment

   e. Time management

   f. Employee compensation

Solutions to the above questions can be downloaded from the **Online Resources** *section of this book on* **www.vibrantpublishers.com**

This page is intentionally left blank

Chapter 9

Health And Safety Development

This chapter focusses more pointedly on the health aspect of regulatory compliance.

Readers will discover the following:

- The role of health safety and development in an organization, and the likely results of an organization that does not practice proper health and safety management

- Requirements for a conducive work environment

- HRM relevance in ensuring work safety in an organization

- Appropriate practices to put in place for enhanced health and safety in the workplace

An employee in an organization may underperform as a result of poor health. This is likely to be the case when an organization does too little or nothing about its health system. Further, an unhealthy working environment is noncompliant with any legal, regulatory system. An organization that does not practice a proper health and safety management system may likely face lawful charges in a jurisdiction.

When attention is paid to the health sector, it does a lot of good, beginning from encouraging employees to perform brilliantly. It equally attracts and retains top talent in an organization for better productivity.

An establishment with no health and safety approach may just be steps away from a breakdown to disaster. For instance, carelessness to a broken cable in an organization may result in a shock that can hospitalize an employee. If care is not taken about such, a life or lives might be lost, which is the most detrimental effect for any company.

The practice of a proper health and safety management system would ensure not just a compliant health scheme but will boost the chances of an employee or workforce not getting hurt while in action. This approach will cut down harmful circumstances that expose employees to mental or physical injury.

The health management approach will further ensure that a checkup is continuously done in a bid to keep the environment injury-free. Moreover, this health management is not just about environmental sanitation but the presence of a good and a sound environment for duties to take place. It concerns even the employer-employee relationship as well as its relationship with the growth of the business.

On a scale of 10, about 6.1 counts of organizations practice a proper health management approach, which is proactive. The remaining count practices a curative approach that may be active or partially inactive. An active practice exposes the employee to emotional or physical harm, and this will likely affect the organization in two ways:

- Low production

- Possible regulatory noncompliant punishment

A low producing company will be suppressed by a high producing company and may be forced to succumb to pressure in a short while. On the other hand, company policies towards mental and physical health that do not comply with the legal principles of the jurisdiction may suffer a legal critique. The company may have to either plan a proper health management system in the process or face the wrath of the law for carelessness towards employee conditions.

9.1 Requirements for a Safe Work Environment

An organization is responsible for a safe employee working environment. For an employer to know how correct the health practices of the organization are, such an employer should refer to the health management guidelines as stated by the legal and regulatory principles. Also, the mentioned guidelines must be duly practiced to ensure the sound emotional and physical health of employees.

In this section, however, the basic requirements for a safe work environment will be identified, such that an employer should not find it difficult to comprehend.

Compliance with Standard Legal Principles

There will be a safe work environment where there is a strategic plan for legal compliance. An employer must ensure that there is a constant review of the regulatory principles of the law of the justification. If health policies do not conform to the stated principles, then there is a problem. For most organizations, the approved legal and regulatory guidelines are the norms to know when health practice in a workplace is sound. The HRM department reviews and ensures that the company's health practice is in line with a stated legal Act.

Availability of Safety Tools

The scope of managing safety and health in an organization is extremely broad. There are specific safety tools that must be made readily available in an organization. A few, among the many, include hazard amplifiers, emotional check programs, and safety programs. This brief list is far from all-inclusive and should be explored more thoroughly based on industry, job types, facilities, jurisdiction (state and local laws), and more.

Regular Supervision of Workplace

The physical outlook or nature of a business environment must be regularly supervised. Supervision is a way to maintain regulatory compliance with the required standards of health management. A company may employ the services of a professional or an agency to examine and fix portions of the business environment that pose a risk to human health. Many organizations employ a Risk Management or a Health and Risk Management division or department. This particular department can sometimes be a sub-unit of Human Resources, or function independently.

The Utility of Warning Signs

There must be warning signs or symbols placed in relevant places to caution every employee of a danger. These signs must be printed in visible colors for easy detection.

Records of Employee Injuries

It is required that an employer make a file for recording employee data for those who suffer hazardous damages or injury in the company.

Indiscriminate Treatment of Employees

Employees who duly complain about the deprivation of their rights must not be discriminated against. Every employee holds the right to disagree with unfavorable policies of a company. It is sound practice to invite such employee(s) to communicate their concerns and explore solutions to resolve the problems.

Adoption of Health Programs

There should be informative and relevant programs targeted at health improvement in the workplace. Such programs should range from the effectiveness of communication, the need to abide by the internal and external policies, what and what not to do with regards to health, how to manage the work tools and the utility of hazard amplifiers such as fire extinguisher or AED (automated external defibrillator).

Figure 9.1

9.2 Roles of HRM in Safety Development

HRM is a vital organ in safety development and management. Safety is one of the primary roles of HRM, and this is the case in several modern organizations. HRM is known to be responsible for the overall growth of a company, and one of the many managerial aspects that lead to this growth is safety. An unsound business environment is not a healthy ground. Such an environment may feature conflict among employees, groups, and management. Furthermore, there may be the presence of an emotional breakdown, which affects an individual's performance, thereby resulting in low production. In short, a company risks losing the prowess to maintain its highly competitive level.

Below are the primary roles of HRM in safety development in any organization:

Provision of Medical Examination

It is the responsibility of HRM to provide medical examinations for its employees. This serves as a checkup for employees' health and to ensure that affected employees are cared for. Lately, in industries, there were cases of employees suffering industrial damages ranging from low sperm count, gradual deafness, high blood pressure, broken joints, and other ailments. These were results from working with toxic wastes and handling heavy-duty equipment. The management on their part did not pay attention to the health of such employees who later struggle with unyielding treatments. Employees exposed to and subject to such poor conditions and who are not afforded the benefit of regular medical examinations often live shorter lifespans. This may be avoided when employers examine their employees regularly to appropriately promote good health, safety, and working conditions - which will also serve as a boost in production.

Ensuring Legal Health Compliance

HRM manages compliance duties. They have to learn and get trained on newly effective regulatory policies with regard to employee health, both physically and mentally. They just ensure that a company operates in conformation with the established principles and that no employee is discriminated against. This compliance practice is necessary to prevent unnecessary expenses resulting from legal charges.

Keeping Communication Alive with Employees

Lack of proper communication in the workplace is toxic. It could easily lead to a misunderstanding among employees and management or employers. Conflict arises when there is a lack of communication. Such conflict could be intraindividual, intergroup, and intragroup conflict. It often discourages a proper passage of information, and every member of the organization suffers from poor, lacking, or miscommunication. The HRM must be proactive or reactive in time to avoid any such conflict from escalating.

Health Programs

This informs both employers and employees that each has a role in ensuring proper health management. It could be discussions about the need for effective communication, commitment, and the need to reward deserving employees. Health programs are also a strong incentive for employees who seek out differentiators among potential employers. They are not only an exceptional recruitment tool, but sound strategy in retention, maintaining employee health, keeping up productivity, and building sound employer-employee relationships.

9.3 Strategies to Promote Employee's Health and Safety

A proper strategy must undergo scientific approaches. If a planned strategy is not scientific, it will contain glitches that may foil the entire plan. This said, it is vital to practice a healthy standard in a business environment to boost productivity. Beginning from how individuals interact in the workplace, healthiness matters. Also, an organization must always be careful when issuing hazardous items to employees to work with. Such employees must be duly trained on how to handle such equipment and must be experienced in the field; otherwise, professionals should be hired for the task.

Lots of organizations suffer legal problems. This results from the lack of working strategies that manage employee health in a manner that complies with legal and regulatory principles. Planning a strategy that works is not expensive. Follow the below four-step strategic plan in order to excellently promote employee's health and safety.

Step 1 — Study the Situation

The first step is to study the situation. One way to study the situation and come up with an accurate problem to solve is to question the workforce. Management may not be perfect in detecting problems. Employees are more exposed to the activities and may better understand what problem must be fixed to help with health management. In cases where it is difficult to sort the situation internally, a company may alternatively hire experts to examine the situation.

Step 2 — Formulate Health Policies

Making internal policies that do not conflict with regulatory laws should always be an option. After detecting a problematic source, a policy formulation follow-up should be conducted. This process involves simple strategic planning that aims at proffering solutions to mental or physical health issues. For instance, if the health problem is related to emotional problems involving a team of employees, such a team should be relieved of the responsibility or specific roles apportioned to each and individual with instruction on what to do. This way, there will be no call for opposition among the team on whose objective is more brilliant. However, it is good to invite each of the team members and learn their own ideas.

Step 3 — Introduce Health Programs

Health in the workforce is not just about environmental health but employee and non-environmental health-related issues like personal conflict and opposing ideas. Introduce mandatory health issue programs and make the present health problem a focal point of the discussion. In cases of environmental health, instruct and teach employees how best to handle work tools, the importance of obeying cautious signs, and how to use the available protective tools during a burst out of disaster such as fire outbreak.

Step 4 — Emphasis

Training employees may not be enough to create solutions. Therefore, ensure an every-time emphasis on the benefits of sound health, ranging from employee relationships, environmental hazards, and the need to curb toxic emotions in the workplace. Train and encourage employees to be committed and self-disciplined. There are various ways of encouraging employees, and one such is the issuance of reward to excellently performing employees.

Chapter Summary

◆ Health safety and development boosts the morale of the workforce in an organization.

◆ HRM persons should not fail to be attentive to the health faculty of the organization.

◆ The requirements for a safe working environment include the availability of safety tools, supervision of workplace, utility of warning signs, records of employee injuries, indiscriminate treatment of employees, and adoption of health programs.

◆ There are several plans HRM should consider mapping out to promote or enhance employee's health.

Quiz 9

1. Which of the following is not considered a primary role of HRM in the safety development of an organization?

   a. Ensuring legal health compliance

   b. Health programs

   c. Maintaining Communication with Employees

   d. Providing an onsite health and wellness clinic

2. _____ are an incentive for employees who are looking for differences in potential employers.

   a. Employee relations

   b. Employee communication

   c. Health programs

   d. Health hazards

3. **Select the series of words that represent the correct order for implementing a strategic plan to promote employee's health and safety.**

    a. Study situation, formulate policies, introduce programs, emphasize

    b. Formulate policies, study situation, emphasize, introduce programs

    c. Formulate policies, emphasize, study situation, introduce programs

    d. Study situation, emphasize, formulate policies, introduce programs

4. **There are (3) primary safety tools that should be available in any organization. [True or False]**

    a. True

    b. False

5. **A(n) _____ working environment is noncompliant with any legal, regulatory system.**

    a. secure

    b. safe

    c. unhealthy

    d. open space

Solutions to the above questions can be downloaded from the **Online Resources** *section of this book on*
www.vibrantpublishers.com

Chapter 10

People Development

The focal point of this chapter is on development, and more precisely, the development of the workforce. The subject reveals correlated concepts including employee development, personal development, workforce development, and people development.

Chapter ten covers the following concepts:

- Employee development

- The definition of people development

- The makeup of people development

- What people development attempts to achieve in an organization

- Why it is necessary to implement the concept in an organization

- The various working strategies of people development

- A broad overview of how training, coaching, and mentoring work in HRM

Employee development has, for a while, become a prominent commitment and goal in most progressive organizations. This concerns every area of the organization but pays particular attention to the mental and physical growth of employees.

People development is a series of attempts, moves, and bids by management to grow its workforce. This scope can be said to be a strategic plan towards achieving a goal or bringing a potential goal into actuality. The primary aim of this facet of management is to build employees and equip them with the necessary knowledge required to run the business.

Employee development is the cardinal thread that controls how an organization performs at the end of the day. People development studies individuals, re-studies them, and appraise such individuals. This insinuates that it is not just about employees becoming better, but that such employees have undergone various scrutinizing examinations. Employees are not always aware of this aspect of their employment. However, there is always that consciousness that someone is watching and that such a person requires more. Nevertheless, when the organization does not hint at recognizing an employee, whether by rewarding for excellence or simply acknowledging, such an employee may not be responsive to the onboard developmental strategies.

In essence, people development is implicitly an act of tuning employees to become individually better. It is about uncovering all the technical aspects of the business to the employees. It involves training through seminars, company-sponsored educative programs, and awareness campaigns.

The Makeup of People Development

People Development is a Science

Any developing strategy must be scientific. Consider a learning institution, for instance. Everything that is done is in accordance with science to achieve successful learning. Beginning from the proprietor, there is a hierarchical order of the management. In the learning aspect, which is the primary developmental aspect, there is a time-based study, with each course having its period. This is scientific because it involves order, manner of approach, and methodology. This is also the basis of people development in any organization. To sum this constituent, an employer's attitude towards employees is a major determinant of employee responsiveness to the developmental attempts.

It is Vital and Effective

People development is not a legal or compliance requirement, but it is vital for all-round development. It does not have to be forced on the system because it is a scope that naturally permeates the existence of an organization. Should the organization fight for a place of recognition in the business sphere? Should the workforce be motivated to do better? Most HR and business professionals would propose, yes. Then, this is why people development is vital, and it can be useful if done well. Remember, this system implemented with a scientific approach to maximize success.

It Takes Time

It generally does not take long to become fully effective. It is the innate abilities of an employee that determine how long or how short it will take for the system to become effective. This is more like using the term 'adaptation.' Not all employees will adapt quickly to developmental approaches. Some may require a little more time and even encouragement to do so. Encouraging an employee makes them want to go all-out to become better for a company. It could be such that they invest time and money in online courses and other external training just to learn and become better.

Employees Love It

In an establishment that deals with online promotion, web management, and blogging, Search Engine Optimization (SEO) is a must-know technique. A recruit who knows too little about SEO will perform poorly in such a field. However, offering to drill such an employee will not just make him or her happy, but also encouraged.

Figure 10.1

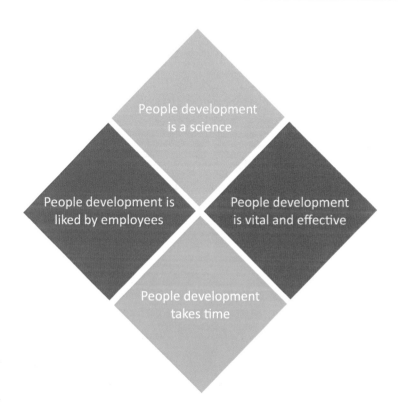

10.1 Objectives of People Development

Developing individuals serving in an organization is often targeted at yielding overall organizational improvement. The objective is simple, and it deals solely with the overall increment in outputs. If placed side by side, it will be noted that an organization practicing the art of people development performs at least two times better than the counterpart expecting employees to know all. The goal or objectives of people development is quite easy to comprehend. The task for HR is to make employee's development a focal point for the sustained growth of the company. There are a few other focal areas that a people development systems target.

These include:

Performance Excellence

People development targets performance because performance determines the success of an organization or attainment of a fixed goal. Without a high level of performance, an organization will likely underperform. In order to prevent underperformance from employees, employing the people development system will look to solve the problem. It, therefore, means that employee development targets building an individual to become an influential force in the performance faculty of an organization.

Skills Improvement

Having a newly recruited staff requires attentiveness to such staff. If such staff is allowed to develop by learning from what he or she finds around their job environment, adaptation will take days. This means that productivity from that angle will suffer a setback. It is also on this note that the employee or people development system targets a quick skills improvement of such individuals.

Innovativeness

HR should be more focused on employee skills because some of the employees are capable of introducing techniques that could help in the company's development. With the integration of a proper people development or management system, such employees could be easily identified and explored. As such, the aspect of the individual system in question here (people development) targets the creation of room for employee innovativeness.

Quicker Adaptation

Practically, it takes quite a long time for recruits to adapt. Studies show that the first adaption an employee undergoes is environmental adaptation. This is such that individual attempts to get used to her workplace before transiting into understanding the nature of the job. After understanding the nature of the job, an employee will try to acquaint herself with organizational policies before getting to learn from colleagues. All of these will cost time and does not sit well with the progress of the company. People development then comes in shoots towards causing the individual to adapt in no time. This is also applicable to employees who witness changes in their workplaces.

10.2 Importance of People Development

The importance of people development is primarily the enhancement of employees' competence for the collective good of the organization. There are two strong views or perspectives surrounding people development. While some critics argue that the entire system is based solely on organizational development and not employees' benefit, others argue that it directly benefits employees.

One such view that supports the argument that the development system benefits an organization rather than its employees is Chay et al.'s (2003) position that employee development is a perceived investment in employees that benefits an organization by issuing it a competitive advantage over competitors. The nature of this opinion stresses that people development system focuses on building employees to fertilize an organization with little or no sufficient gain on their part.

For the second view, several perspectives in books, journals, websites, libraries, articles, and magazines propose that people development is of importance to both employees and employers. In general, let's consider the central importance of this system of development with regards to employees' performance and the organization's productivity.

Employee Self-Growth

This agrees with the views of critics on stances that people development is two-sided. The perspective is that this developmental system equally profits the employees of an organization. Such a concept is not far from the truth because employees do not learn to store in the brain of an organization but in theirs. What an organization expects in return is just the application of such acquired skills, coupled with intelligence for better results. To an extent, an organization that trains its workforce through specific developmental programs is only doing such an individual a favor. In essence, people development builds individuals to become a marketable workforce in the labor sphere. Such opportune employees often become bosses of their own after a few months or years of gathering experiences.

Improved Employer-Employee Relationship

Many argue that any developmental system aimed at an organization's development creates an environment where employees and their employers interact. Depending on the personality of an employer, the employee may be fortunate to have a friendly and casual relationship with the employer. This makes the training more interesting. The employee would also be able to communicate, inform, and advise his or her boss on what may or may not be right for the company. The best developmental process often features various interactive sessions. When there is a dull learning atmosphere, the developing pace of an individual may decline rapidly.

Timely Production

The goal of development is to build, and the building is targeted at something. HR designs this system to improve employees in a manner that hastens production for quicker deliveries. An example is the training that McDonald's employee goes through to serve fast. The faster the employee, the more customers to be served. The more customers served means more money before a competitor contacts such available buyer for the same business. Moreover, while speedy production might be the case, quality matters. As such, employees trained to work fast should also apply intelligence for quality.

Competition Among Employees

Interorganizational competitions are often costly. One such cause is the cost of an advertisement, which is necessary for competitors to remain popular. Although competition makes organizations lose money in a bid or harvest for clients, it ensures a compelling sort of competition, which is what everyone hopes for.

10.3 Effective People Development Strategies

Development is synonymous with growth. Growth on its own simply refers to a progressive increase in the nature, size, scope, and abilities of something. It could be emotional, financial, as well as physical growth.

In modern organizations, growth management is the key to a gainful performance. For this growth to occur, there must be scientifically planned developmental actions. Effective development strategies follow due processes without which an objective may be nulled. Therefore, it is not necessary but crucial to adopt a methodological process towards achieving an effective development.

It is consequential to abandon the thoughts of the effectiveness of people development on an organization and its employees. Note that employees will develop but will not develop fast without any attempt. Moreover, where an attempt is initiated without a proper strategic plan to guide it, the objective foils right from the start. See section 10.3.1. to 10.3.6. for fully tested, working, and effective development strategies that build employees and enhance performances in any organization.

10.3.1 Professional In-depth Training

Employees do not inherit innate abilities to become impactful. Instead, they are developed and trained to grow their level of impact on an organization. Most organizations use seminars as an attempt to defeat the competitor workforce. It aids in building or molding employees into becoming not just professionals, but impactors or impactful resources. The objective of any such drillings must thrive on propagating confidence among staff. It tugs on the strands of the actual human capital. Training should rely basically on patterning an individual to become self-efficient, able to improvise, and capable of exploring a job role with intelligence.

Professional training and developmental approach bring about a sense of orderliness. It teaches an employee to be groomed and relaxed, especially while working under high pressure.

Some employees do not know how to decide on what and what not to do now or later. This entails their inefficiency in being able to prioritize a duty or a plan of action over another. Another prevalent problem that handshakes with people development is communication. An average untrained or under-developing employee lags in the communicative area. This spans from client communication, employer communication, and even communications with another workforce.

HR should consider the atmospheric conditions of the training program. Atmospheric here refers to both emotional and physical aspects. Where there is a fault or bitterness, such as with a relationship, individual conflicts, hard, theoretical approach, over-seriousness from an employer, it will become challenging for employees to learn. Instead of encouragement, such employees may resort to being discouraged or disorganized.

In essence, strategically employing seminars, professional tutorials, and the like will mold an employee to understand the need to be strategic and workout issues without an external guide.

10.3.2 Coaching and Mentoring

Coaching and mentoring are differing conduits that contribute to the development of an employee. An individual may make efforts to please a company, if not for anything, but for the salary or wages he receives. These two have been practiced and believed to be the closest form of strategic planning, that is, that demands a non-distant communication between employer and employee. However, coaching is the most prevalent system since it does not encourage a sort of 'studies of abilities' the way mentoring does.

Let's contrast these two terms to determine how they function and what an employer or company ought to do about the situation.

Coaching

Let's use a construct that is somewhat familiar to many- the sport, American football. In football, two teams organize against each other. Each team features a head coach, and his responsibility is solely to make his side conquerors. The coach provides elements of oversight, direction, counseling, reprimand, decision-making guidance, and more. On this note, a team without a coach may become disorganized and vulnerable to opposition.

This concept applies to this method of employee development. An employee may not necessarily require a coach, but a coach makes things easier. A coach is a strategist in management. He has to be proactive, study the business environment, and know what duty an employee can do better and should do. As an employer, employee development should be pointed at HR persons.

Why Coaching is Necessary

- Coaching challenges an employee to reach a goal similar to those goals of sports teams

- An employee is tasked with assignments that help to build their abilities

- An employee will understand that he is being watched and would perform well enough to impress

- It bridges the gap that may exist between an employee and his employer

Mentoring

Mentoring as an aspect of development differs from coaching in many ways. It is a practice that makes the management get even closer to employees. Does it get employees closer than coaching? Practically, it does. Mentoring involves the psychology study of an individual. And, for such a study to be fruitful, there must be a closeness that will allow the HR person even to understand what bothers an employee.

Mentoring is not necessary but relevant to an employee's development. It allows an employee to be apportioned the best suitable task, breaches the relationship gap, and makes it easier for an employee to become very functional in a particular field.

Ultimately, the ideas, coaching, and mentoring are great systems of development that should be practiced in modern management. In larger establishments, it is ideal to practice coaching while mentoring will suffice in smaller establishments.

10.3.3 Inter-department Staffing

This has to do with functionality in multiple departments. The nature of jobs has evolved to a point where organizations demand employees with multiple skills. As a trend, several professionals have made it ideal to be versatile in not just a single department but others when the need arises. The development of employees centers around this scope. When employees are placed in positions of learning that introduce them to new skills, they are bound to learn and perfect the art.

Modern-day labor does not consider only a single skill as ideal any longer. Now, the vision demands to have individuals that can operate in multiple job posts and still function professionally well. There is nothing wrong with being multi-skilled, whether the skills are related or not. It is smart for an employee to be skillful in at least two roles. Such an employee stands a chance of earning a positive appraisal and possibly a reward for his performance.

One of the upcoming ways to achieving success in management is frequent role switching. A company with no such practice may not perform well enough whenever the occasion demands a switch in the role.

Pros and Cons of Inter-Department Staffing

Although the pros are many, we will still outline the basic pros and cons of inter-department staffing.

Pros

- The emergence of a multi-skilled worker

- A readily available option

- Multiple replacements

- New job experiences

- A multitasking practice in a company which boosts production

- Progressive company productivity

- Competitiveness among staff

- Dedication to learning for development

Cons

- Overworking of staff

- Extra payment for extra job

- The stress of attempting to crack contrasting responsibilities

Inter-staffing is the proper strategy to employ, especially when there are frequent work changes that demand a replacement and a rapid adaptation.

10.3.4 Cultivate Emotional Intelligence

A strategic approach that fully connects an employee's emotions buys a portion of their thought. Once human resources persons or managers can connect by understanding the more emotional intellectual aspects of an employee, they can take leverage of their abilities and manipulate them to see the need for a more advanced way of handling pressuring tasks.

Emotional intelligence is simply the attentiveness of employers to employees' emotional aspect with regards to how it can be controlled. This involves being conscious of what staff thinks by inquiring into it and how it influences their performance. Employers may not be perfect in controlling the emotional aspect of employees because some of them are very brilliant in concealing emotions. However, cultivating emotional intelligence, in a certain manner of approach, tends to be resolute. Sometimes, employers may not have to be still or hard on employees. For example, while being aware of an employee's emotional status and attitude towards productiveness, employers/managers may become easily vexed, which requires some level of self-control and understanding. Advisably, if lacking the psychological dexterity to manage such sensitiveness, allow the right department or professionals to do so.

10.3.5 Personal Development

Personal development has to do with the individual growth of employees after seminars, webinars, courses, or any training program. This improvement arrives, not because of the need to, but because such an individual is being encouraged to grow within the organization.

After every engagement in drilling for a particular period, an individual will see the need to take over himself from there. That is, to become wholly dependent on his abilities and models of handling tasks instead of depending on what an instructor advises. The employee will get to understand that it is a must to develop and in order to become rightly recognized in the organization. This is usually the case when the manner of the relation is accommodating, for example, when an employee experiences a somewhat soft approach to knowledge acquisition rather than a hard approach.

During the developmental stages and processes, it is recommended that employees be tested to ascertain their progress. A trainee with low interest or a complete disengagement will underperform. However, it will be very unsound to declare such employee(s) as incapable. Instead, look out for the pieces of slumps that orchestrate the concentration of such individuals, and that discourages underperformance.

The downside of an individual's attempt to develop personally is that it allures employees a room to be decisive, which may result in laziness. Personal development rallies around an individual's environment. This appeals severely to the emotions of an individual who wants to do more. As a plan of action, personal development can result from various activities, some of which include:

- Online courses

- Video tutorials

- Extra lessons during free periods

- Questioning of other employees who may have a better knowledge of an objective

The list is endless, and it covers every aspect or perspective that an employee honors to personally develop and become more contributive to the goal set by an organization.

10.3.6 Promotions and Rewards

When individuals work, they expect things other than salaries and wages. In short, workers require recognitions, and these recognitions may arrive as tangible or intangible rewards. The reward could be cash in hand, an item, or a special moment dedicated to such an excellently performing individual.

Promotions and rewards each refer to compensation. However, these terms differ and could as well impact employee performance differently.

Let's assess these terms individually and ascertain their level of relevance to an employee's growth:

Promotions

This could be fixed or variable. It is fixed when an employee and employer meet to negotiate and agree that after a particular goal is attained, such employee will be promoted. On the other hand, variable promotion occurs prior to the employee's awareness. Promotion is simply a shift from a lower to a higher level of responsibility. Promotions do not always come with raises (increased pay), and they charge an employee to become proactive in his or her way of dealing with things.

This strategy was introduced right from the early stage of human laboring. It is such that an employer attempts to lure forward every iota of skills possessed by an individual to the business environment.

Rewards

Rewards may be monetary or non-monetary. It is usually based on a company's willfulness to encourage an employee to do better. It could also fall based on agreement. However, the necessary general idea is that rewards are tricky but costly attempts to get the best out of every individual serving an organization.

Promotions and rewards are generally relevant to boost an employee's engagement. These practices have been commonly utilized by several organizations to achieve employee development at a rapid pace. It is highly recommended to invite these practices into a company and experience enhanced performance, pro-activeness, and intelligible formats of handling every given task in the organization.

Chapter Summary

◆ People development focuses on the growth of human resources for the benefit of the company. If neglected, a company will likely witness a backdrop in its competitiveness as well as in its earnings.

◆ Implementing a working development practice helps companies attain a desired level of productivity and success.

◆ It is important, but not necessary, to employ development practices in a company for the sake of enhanced employee growth which impacts the business positively.

◆ Effective people development strategies include professional in-depth training, coaching and mentoring, inter-department staffing, cultivating emotional intelligence, personal development, and promotions and rewards.

Quiz 10

1. **People development is implicitly an act of tuning employees to become _____ better.**

    a. psychologically

    b. emotionally

    c. collectively

    d. individually

2. **Which is not a focal area of people development?**

    a. Innovativeness

    b. Skills improvement

    c. Quicker adaptation

    d. Performance excellence

    e. None of the above

3. **One view of people development is that the development system benefits _____ rather than _____. An opposing view suggests that it benefits both.**

    a. employees, managers

    b. managers, employees

    c. employees, the employer

    d. the employer, employees

4. Most employees are naturally gifted with inherit innate abilities that allow them to impact an organization, its productivity and its growth significantly. [True or False]

   a. True

   b. False

5. _____ involves the psychology study of an individual. And, for such a study to be fruitful, there must be a closeness that will allow the HR person even to understand what bothers an employee.

   a. Managing

   b. Coaching

   c. Mentoring

   d. Employer-employee relationship

Solutions to the above questions can be downloaded from the **Online Resources** *section of this book on* **www.vibrantpublishers.com**

References

"Bill Gates on Business". Retrieved January 24, 2020, from www.webwriterspotlight.com.

"Carnegie D. Leadership. Retrieved January 22, 2020, from www.dalecarnegie.com/en/courses/leadership-cape-province

"John Quincy Adams' Quote". Retrieved January 21, 2020, from www.google.com/amp/s/quoteinvestigator.com/2011/07/03/inspire-dream-leader/amp/.

"Mohammad Ali's Quote on Obedience". Retrieved January 27, 2020 from www.quotefancy.com.

"Paul Koziarz, CSI President and General Manager of Regulatory Compliance on Managing Compliance". Retrieved January 25, 2020, from www.compliancebridge.com

"President John F. Kennedy on the Alliance for Progress". www.goooglereads.com. Retrieved 23 January 2020.

Alpkan, Lutfihak & Bulut, Cagri & Gunday, Gurhan & Ulusoy, Gunduz & Kilic, Kemal. (2010). Organizational support for intrapreneurship and its interaction with human capital to enhance innovative performance. Management Decision. 48. 732-755.10.1108/02517471080000697.

Amele, M. (November 17, 2017). Re: Effective business management skills for beginners. Retrieved January 23, 2020, from www.trainingzone.co.uk/community/blogs/markamele/effective-business-management-skills-for-beginners.

Austin, D. (1976). Conflict: A more professional approach *Personnel Administrator*. Retrieved January 27, 2020. doi: 10.1177/105960117900400406.

Bauer, S. and Maylander, A. (1919). The Road to the Eight-Hour Day. *Monthly Labour Review*, 9(2), 41-65. Retrieved January 19, 2020, from www.jstor.org/stable/41827595.

Beach, D. (1980). Personnel: the management of people at work. New York: Macmillan.

Beckhard, R. (1969). Organization Development: strategies and models. United States: Reading, Mass, Addison-Wesley.

Bell, A. (2002). *Six ways to resolve workplace conflicts*. San Francisco: CA: University of San Francisco.

Benjamin, A., Campbell, C. and Kryscynski (2012). Rethinking Sustained Competitive Advantage from Human Capital. *Academy of Management Review*. Vol. 37. Retrieved January 21, 2020, from www.joirnals.aom.org.

Burke, W. (1982). Organization development principles and practices. United States: Scott, Foresman.

Chay Hoon Lee and Norman T. Bruvold, (2003). 'Creating value for employees: investment in employee development, Int. J. of Human Resource Management Vol.14 No.6 p981-1000.

Cummings, T. and Worley, C. (1997). Organization Development and Change. (6th Edition). United States: South-Western College Pub.

Davies, K. (1984). Law of compulsory purchase and compensation. London: Butterworth.

DeCenzo, D and Robbins, S. (1999). Human resource management. New Jersey, United States: Wiley.

Essays, UK. (November 2018). Benefits and Strategies of Performance Management. Retrieved from https://www.ukessays.com/essays/management/armstrong-and-baron-define-performance-management.php?vref=1

Flippo, E. (1980). Personnel management. (Ed. 5) New York: McGraw-Hill.

Flippo, E. (2007). Personnel management. 6th ed. New York: McGraw-Hill.

Hart, B. (2009). Conflict in the workplace. Behavioral Consultants, P.C. Retrieved from Excelatlife.com

Hart, B. (2009). *Conflict in the workplace.* Behavioural Consultants, P.C. Retrieved from www.excelatlife.com/articles/conflict_at_work.htm.

Legge, K. (1995). HRM and 'strategic' integration with business policy. In: Human Resource Management. Management, Work and Organisations: Palgrave, London.

Lockett, J. (1992). Effective Performance Management: A Strategic Guide to Getting the Best People. Lincoln, United Kingdom: Kogan Page Ltd.

Mayo, E. (1949). *Hawthrone* and the western electric company. Public Administration: Concepts and Cases, 149-158.

Moore. M. H. (1995). *Creating public value: Strategy management in government.* Boston, MA: Havard University Press.

Perlroth, Nicole. (October 3, 2017). The New York Times: All 3 billion Yahoo accounts were affected by 2013. Retrieved January 30, 2020, from www.nytimes.com.

Smriti Chand. Conflict Management: characteristics, types, stages, causes and other details. Retrieved January 29, 2020 from www.yourarticlelibrary.com/business/conflict-management-characteristics-types-stages-causes-and-other-details-5431.

Stiglitz, J. (2007). *The Right to Know: Transparency for an Open World* (Florini A, Ed.). Columbia University Press. Retrieved January 31, 2020, from www.jstor.org/stable/10.7312/flor14158.

Taylor, F. (1911). The principles of scientific management. New York, NY, USA and London, UK: Harper & Brothers.

Thomas, K. and Kilman, R. (1974). The Thomas-Kilman Conflict Mode Instrument (Mountain View, CA: CPP, Inc.).

Yoder, D. (1970). Personnel management and industrial relations. Upper Saddle River, New Jersey, America: Prentice-Hall.

Noe, R., Hollenbeck, J., Gerhart, B., and Wright P. (2009). Fundamentals of Human Resources Management: Third Edition. New York, New York: McGraw-Hill Irwin.

Made in the USA
Columbia, SC
08 August 2024

3ab58f4b-b26d-451e-98a5-165929b1059fR02